Six Poets of the Great War

Edited by Adrian Barlow

Series Editor: Judith Baxter

CAMBRIDGE
UNIVERSITY PRESS

The publishers would like to thank Nicholas McGuinn and Jane Ogborn for their help as consulting editors for the series.

Published by the Press Syndicate of the University of Cambridge
The Pitt Building, Trumpington Street, Cambridge CB2 1RP
40 West 20th Street, New York, NY 10011–4211, USA
10 Stamford Road, Oakleigh, Melbourne 3166, Australia

First published 1995

Printed in Great Britain by Scotprint, Musselburgh, Scotland

A catalogue record for this book is available from the British Library

ISBN 0 521 48569 X paperback

Prepared for publication by Stenton Associates

CONTENTS

———————————— ✦ ————————————

Section C: Wilfred Owen

Section D: Siegfried Sassoon

Section E: Edmund Blunden

Section F: Richard Aldington

Section G: Further Poems

CAMBRIDGE LITERATURE

This edition of *Six Poets of the Great War* is part of the Cambridge Literature series, and has been specially prepared for students in schools and colleges who are studying the book as part of their English course.

This study edition invites you to think about what happens when you read a poem, and it suggests that you are not passively responding to words on the page which have only one agreed interpretation, but that you are actively exploring and making new sense of what you read. Your 'reading' will partly stem from you as an individual, from your own experiences and point of view, and to this extent your interpretation will be distinctively your own. But your reading will also stem from the fact that you belong to a culture and a community, rooted in a particular time and place. So, your understanding may have much in common with that of others in your class or study group.

There is a parallel between the way you read this book and the way the poems in it were written. The Resource Notes at the back are devised to help you to investigate the complex nature of the writing process. This begins with the poet's first, tentative ideas and sources of inspiration, moves through to the stages of writing, production and publication, and ends with the text's reception by the reading public, reviewers, critics and students. So the general approach to study focuses on five key questions:

Who has written these poems and why?

What type of texts are these poems?

How were these poems produced?

How do these poems present their subject?

Who reads them? How do they interpret them?

The text of *Six Poets of the Great War* is presented complete and uninterrupted. You will find some words in the text asterisked: these are words which may be unfamiliar because they have a particular cultural or linguistic significance. They are explained in the Glossary section at the back.

The Resource Notes encourage you to take an active and imaginative approach to studying poetry both in and out of the classroom. As well as providing you with information about many aspects of *Six Poets of the Great War* they offer a wide choice of activities to work on individually, or in groups. Above all, they give you the chance to explore this interesting collection in a variety of ways: as a reader, an actor, a researcher, a critic, and a writer.

Judith Baxter

INTRODUCTION

War poetry has become one of the best-known types of poetry in the twentieth century. The First World War was largely responsible for this. Not only did it provoke an extraordinary outpouring of poetry of all kinds and quality, it also gave so many young practising poets first-hand experience of war in a way that had never occurred in earlier conflicts.

This book does not pretend to be an anthology. It presents a selection of writing by six poets who happened also to become soldiers. Three of them were killed during the Great War; three survived. Two, Wilfred Owen and Siegfried Sassoon, are still today very well-known, though for most people their reputation rests on a small number of poems. Two more, Isaac Rosenberg and Edmund Blunden, are also well-known, by name at least. Of the other two, Edward Thomas wrote poems that are strongly affected by the war but which do not attempt to describe life and death on the Western Front. His reputation as a poet and as a major figure in modern poetry continues to grow, but many people would not think of him as a war poet at all. Richard Aldington, by contrast, was highly regarded as a war poet and novelist during the 1920s and 1930s, but his reputation today has faded and his poems are out of print.

One aim of this book is to encourage readers to question assumptions about what is or is not a war poem and who is or is not a war poet. Since many people's assumptions are based on such a tiny selection of poems, e.g. Rupert Brooke's 'The Soldier' and Wilfred Owen's 'Strange Meeting', it is important for readers to ask whether different selections of poems would produce different ideas about war poetry. A second aim is to recover poems which are in danger of being lost, but which can add much to our understanding of how poets reacted to war before they started to fight, while they were fighting and when they afterwards came to relive their experiences through poetry. It is a mistake to assume that all the important war poems had been written by the time the Armistice came into effect on 11 November 1918. A third aim is to encourage readers to compare poems and poets, to discover how frequently one can illuminate another.

In recent years a great deal of interest has centred on the writing of poets who were not combatants: the importance of poetry written by women during the Great War, for example, is now much better understood. Between 1914 and 1918 many women experienced conditions near to the Western Front through their work as volunteer ambulance drivers and nurses. Others – mothers, wives, girlfriends, sisters – remained at home with their feelings of helplessness, loss and grief. Some of the finest poems to explore these feelings are only now beginning to be widely known.

In addition to the poems by the six featured poets, this book contains a section of supplementary poems. Some are by other soldier poets, Ivor Gurney, Robert Graves, Herbert Read. Others are by men and women whose writing helps to provide a context within which readers can begin to make their own judgements about war poetry. Where possible, the selections of poems by the six poets also contain at least one or two poems written before the poets became soldiers. Each poem is dated, either by the year of its composition or by the year of its first publication in a collection by the poet.

The Glossary and Notes provide a brief guide to some of the difficult words and phrases in the poems, as well as to some of the historical and geographical references. These are followed by commentaries and suggested activities and topics for discussion. All have one overriding purpose: to encourage readers, whether or not encountering war poetry for the first time, to explore their own responses (and those of other people) to poems which can still speak with as much urgency and poignancy today as when they were written.

Adrian Barlow

SECTION A
Edward Thomas

SECTION A: Poems by Edward Thomas

◆

Fifty Faggots

There they stand, on their ends, the fifty faggots
That once were underwood of hazel and ash
In Jenny Pinks's Copse. Now, by the hedge
Close packed, they make a thicket fancy alone
Can creep through with the mouse and wren. Next Spring   5
A blackbird or a robin will nest there,
Accustomed to them, thinking they will remain
Whatever is for ever to a bird:
This Spring it is too late; the swift has come.
'Twas a hot day for carrying them up: 10
Better they will never warm me, though they must
Light several Winters' fires. Before they are done
The war will have ended, many other things
Have ended, maybe, that I can no more
Foresee or more control than robin and wren.   15

                                    1915

In Memoriam [Easter 1915]

The flowers left thick at nightfall in the wood
This Eastertide call into mind the men,
Now far from home, who, with their sweethearts, should
Have gathered them and will do never again.

                                    1915

The Owl

Downhill I came, hungry, and yet not starved;
Cold, yet had heat within me that was proof
Against the North wind: tired, yet so that rest
Had seemed the sweetest thing under a roof.

Then at the inn I had food, fire, and rest,   5
Knowing how hungry, cold, and tired was I.
All of the night was quite barred out except
An owl's cry, a most melancholy cry

Shaken out long and clear upon the hill,
No merry note, nor cause of merriment,   10
But one telling me plain what I escaped
And others could not, that night, as in I went.

And salted was my food, and my repose,
Salted and sobered,° too, by the bird's voice
Speaking for all who lay under the stars,   15
Soldiers and poor, unable to rejoice.

1915

A Private°

This ploughman dead in battle slept out of doors
Many a frosty night, and merrily
Answered staid drinkers, good bedmen, and all bores:
'At Mrs Greenland's Hawthorn Bush,'° said he,
'I slept.' None knew which bush. Above the town,   5
Beyond 'The Drover', a hundred spot the down°
In Wiltshire. And where now at last he sleeps
More sound in France – that, too, he secret keeps.

1915

This is No Case of Petty Right or Wrong

This is no case of petty right or wrong
That politicians or philosophers
Can judge. I hate not Germans, nor grow hot
With love of Englishmen, to please newspapers.
Beside my hate for one fat patriot°   5
My hatred of the Kaiser° is love true: –
A kind of god he is, banging a gong.
But I have not to choose between the two,
Or between justice and injustice. Dinned
With war and argument I read no more   10
Than in the storm smoking along the wind
Athwart the wood. Two witches' cauldrons roar.
From one the weather shall rise clear and gay;
Out of the other an England beautiful
And like her mother that died yesterday.   15
Little I know or care if, being dull,
I shall miss something that historians
Can rake out of the ashes when perchance
The phoenix broods serene above their ken.°
But with the best and meanest Englishmen   20
I am one in crying, God save England, lest
We lose what never slaves and cattle blessed.
The ages made her that made us from the dust:
She is all we know and live by, and we trust
She is good and must endure, loving her so: 25
And as we love ourselves we hate her foe.

                                                    1915

There was a Time

There was a time when this poor frame was whole
And I had youth and never another care,
Or none that should have troubled a strong soul.
Yet, except sometimes in a frosty air
When my heels hammered out a melody   5
From pavements of a city left behind,
I never would acknowledge my own glee
Because it was less mighty than my mind
Had dreamed of. Since I could not boast of strength
Great as I wished, weakness was all my boast.   10
I sought yet hated pity till at length
I earned it. Oh, too heavy was the cost.
But now that there is something I could use
My youth and strength for, I deny the age,
The care and weakness that I know – refuse   15
To admit I am unworthy of the wage
Paid to a man who gives up eyes and breath
For what can neither ask nor heed his death.

                                          1916

The Sun Used to Shine

The sun used to shine while we two° walked
Slowly together, paused and started
Again, and sometimes mused, sometimes talked
As either pleased, and cheerfully parted

Each night. We never disagreed   5
Which gate to rest on. The to be
And the late past we gave small heed.
We turned from men or poetry

To rumours of the war remote
Only till both stood disinclined   10
For aught but the yellow flavorous coat
Of an apple wasps had undermined;

Or a sentry of dark betonies,
The stateliest of small flowers on earth,
At the forest verge; or crocuses   15
Pale purple as if they had their birth

In sunless Hades° fields. The war
Came back to mind with the moonrise
Which soldiers in the east afar
Beheld then. Nevertheless, our eyes   20

Could as well imagine the Crusades°
Or Caesar's battles.° Everything
To faintness like those rumours fades –
Like the brook's water glittering

Under the moonlight – like those walks   25
Now – like us two that took them, and
The fallen apples, all the talks
And silences – like memory's sand

When the tide covers it late or soon,
And other men through other flowers   30
In those fields under the same moon
Go talking and have easy hours.
                            1916

Roads

I love roads:
The goddesses that dwell
Far along invisible
Are my favourite gods.

Roads go on   5
While we forget, and are
Forgotten like a star
That shoots and is gone.

On this earth 'tis sure
We men have not made   10
Anything that doth fade
So soon, so long endure:

The hill road wet with rain
In the sun would not gleam
Like a winding stream   15
If we trod it not again.

They are lonely
While we sleep, lonelier
For lack of the traveller
Who is now a dream only.   20

From dawn's twilight
And all the clouds like sheep
On the mountains of sleep
They wind into the night.

The next turn may reveal   25
Heaven: upon the crest
The close pine clump, at rest
And black, may Hell conceal.

Often footsore, never
Yet of the road I weary,   30
Though long and steep and dreary
As it winds on for ever.

Helen◇ of the roads,
The mountain ways of Wales
And the Mabinogion◇ tales,   35
Is one of the true gods,

Abiding in the trees,
The threes and fours so wise,
The larger companies,
That by the roadside be,   40

And beneath the rafter
Else uninhabited
Excepting by the dead;
And it is her laughter

At morn and night I hear   45
When the thrush cock sings
Bright irrelevant things,
And when the chanticleer◇

Calls back to their own night
Troops that make loneliness   50
With their light footsteps' press,
As Helen's own are light.

Now all roads lead to France
And heavy is the tread
Of the living; but the dead   55
Returning lightly dance:

Whatever the road bring
To me or take from me,
They keep me company
With their pattering,   60

Crowding the solitude
Of the loops over the downs,
Hushing the roar of towns
And their brief multitude.
                    1916

'Home'

Fair was the morning, fair our tempers, and
We had seen nothing fairer than that land,
Though strange, and the untrodden snow that made
Wild of the tame, casting out all that was
Not wild and rustic and old; and we were glad.   5

Fair too was afternoon, and first to pass
Were we that league° of snow, next the north wind.

There was nothing to return for except need.
And yet we sang nor ever stopped for speed,
As we did often with the start behind.   10
Faster still strode we when we came in sight
Of the cold roofs where we must spend the night.

Happy we had not been there, nor could be,
Though we had tasted sleep and food and fellowship
Together long.
            'How quick,' to someone's lip   15
The word came, 'will the beaten horse run home.'

The word 'home' raised a smile in us all three,
And one repeated it, smiling just so
That all knew what he meant and none would say.
Between three counties far apart that lay   20
We were divided and looked strangely each
At the other, and we knew we were not friends
But fellows in a union that ends
With the necessity for it, as it ought.

Never a word was spoken, not a thought   25
Was thought, of what the look meant with the word
'Home' as we walked and watched the sunset blurred.
And then to me the word, only the word,
'Homesick', as it were playfully occurred:
No more. If I should ever more admit   30
Than the mere word I could not endure it
For a day longer: this captivity
Must somehow come to an end, else I should be
Another man, as often now I seem,
Or this life be only an evil dream.   35

                                        1916

Bugle Call

'No one cares less than I,
Nobody knows but God
Whether I am destined to lie
Under a foreign clod'
Were the words I made to the bugle call in the morning.   5

But laughing, storming, scorning,
Only the bugles know
What the bugles say in the morning,
And they do not care, when they blow
The call that I heard and made words to early this morning. 10

                                        1916

As the Team's Head Brass

As the team's head brass° flashed out on the turn
The lovers disappeared into the wood.
I sat among the boughs of the fallen elm
That strewed an angle of the fallow, and
Watched the plough narrowing a yellow square   5
Of charlock.° Every time the horses turned
Instead of treading me down, the ploughman leaned
Upon the handles to say or ask a word,
About the weather, next about the war.
Scraping the share° he faced towards the wood,   10
And screwed along the furrow till the brass flashed
Once more.
        The blizzard felled the elm whose crest
I sat in, by a woodpecker's round hole,
The ploughman said. 'When will they take it away?'
'When the war's over.' So the talk began –   15
One minute and an interval of ten,
A minute more and the same interval.
'Have you been out?' 'No.' 'And don't want to, perhaps?'
'If I could only come back again, I should.
I could spare an arm. I shouldn't want to lose   20
A leg. If I should lose my head, why, so,
I should want nothing more.... Have many gone
From here?' 'Yes.' 'Many lost?' 'Yes, a good few.
Only two teams work on the farm this year.
One of my mates is dead. The second day   25
In France they killed him. It was back in March,
The very night of the blizzard, too. Now if
He had stayed here we should have moved the tree.'
'And I should not have sat here. Everything
Would have been different. For it would have been   30

Another world.' 'Ay, and a better, though
If we could see all all might seem good.' Then
The lovers came out of the wood again:
The horses started and for the last time
I watched the clods crumble and topple over   35
After the ploughshare and the stumbling team.
                                        1916

Lights Out

I have come to the borders of sleep,
The unfathomable deep
Forest, where all must lose
Their way, however straight
Or winding, soon or late;   5
They can not choose.

Many a road and track
That since the dawn's first crack
Up to the forest brink
Deceived the travellers,   10
Suddenly now blurs,
And in they sink.

Here love ends –
Despair, ambition ends;
All pleasure and all trouble,   15
Although most sweet or bitter,
Here ends, in sleep that is sweeter
Than tasks most noble.

There is not any book
Or face of dearest look   20
That I would not turn from now
To go into the unknown
I must enter, and leave, alone,
I know not how.

The tall forest towers: 25
Its cloudy foliage lowers
Ahead, shelf above shelf:
Its silence I hear and obey
That I may lose my way
And myself.   30

1916

SECTION B
Isaac Rosenberg

SECTION B: Poems by Isaac Rosenberg

◆

In Piccadilly⋄

Lamp-lit faces! to you
What is your starry dew?
Gold flowers of the night
    blue!

Deep in wet pavement's slime,   5
Mud rooted, is your fierce
    prime,
To bloom in lust's coloured
    clime.

The sheen of eyes that lust,   10
Dew, Time made your trust,
Lights your passionless dust.
                    published 1915

The Dead Heroes

Flame out, you glorious
    skies,
Welcome our brave,
Kiss their exultant eyes;
Give what they gave.   5

Flash, mailèd seraphim,⋄
Your burning spears;
New days to outflame their
    dim
Heroic years.   10

Thrills their baptismal tread
The bright proud air;
The embattled plumes out-
　spread
Burn upwards there.　　　　　　　　　15

Flame out, flame out, O
　Song!
Star ring to star,
Strong as our hurt is strong
Our children are.　　　　　　　　　20

Their blood is England's
　heart;
By their dead hands
It is their noble part
That England stands.　　　　　　　　25

England　–　Time gave them
　thee;
They gave back this
To win Eternity
And claim God's kiss.　　　　　　　　30

　　　　　published 1915

The Troop Ship

Grotesque and queerly huddled
Contortionists to twist
The sleepy soul to a sleep,
We lie all sorts of ways
And cannot sleep.   5
The wet wind is so cold,
And the lurching men so careless,
That, should you drop to a doze,
Winds' fumble or men's feet
Are on your face.   10

                    1916

From France

The spirit drank the café lights;
All the hot life that glittered there,
And heard men say to women gay,
'Life is just so in France'.

The spirit dreams of café lights,   5
And golden faces and soft tones,
And hears men groan to broken men,
'This is not Life in France'.

Heaped stones and a charred signboard show
With grass between and dead folk under,   10
And some birds sing, while the spirit takes wing.
And this is Life in France.

                    1916

Marching
(as seen from the left file°)

My eyes catch ruddy necks
Sturdily pressed back –
All a red brick moving glint.
Like flaming pendulums, hands
Swing across the khaki –   5
Mustard-coloured khaki –
To the automatic feet.

We husband the ancient glory
In these bared necks and hands.
Not broke is the forge of Mars;°   10
But a subtler brain beats iron
To shoe the hoofs of death
(Who paws dynamic air now).
Blind fingers loose an iron cloud
To rain immortal darkness   15
On strong eyes.

1916

Break of Day in the Trenches

The darkness crumbles away –
It is the same old druid° Time as ever.
Only a live thing leaps my hand –
A queer sardonic rat –
As I pull the parapet's poppy   5
To stick behind my ear.
Droll rat, they would shoot you if they knew
Your cosmopolitan° sympathies.
Now you have touched this English hand
You will do the same to a German –   10
Soon, no doubt, if it be your pleasure
To cross the sleeping green between.
It seems you inwardly grin as you pass
Strong eyes, fine limbs, haughty athletes
Less chanced than you for life,   15
Bonds to the whims of murder,
Sprawled in the bowels of the earth,
The torn fields of France.
What do you see in our eyes
At the shrieking iron and flame   20
Hurled through still heavens?
What quaver – what heart aghast?
Poppies whose roots are in man's veins
Drop, and are ever dropping;
But mine in my ear is safe,   25
Just a little white with the dust.

                                    1917

Louse Hunting

Nudes – stark and glistening,
Yelling in lurid glee. Grinning faces
And raging limbs
Whirl over the floor one fire.
For a shirt verminously busy   5
Yon soldier tore from his throat, with oaths
Godhead might shrink at, but not the lice.
And soon the shirt was aflare
Over the candle he'd lit while we lay.

Then we all sprang up and stript   10
To hunt the verminous brood.
Soon like a demons' pantomime
The place was raging.
See the silhouettes agape,
See the gibbering shadows   15
Mixed with the battled arms on the wall.
See gargantuan hooked fingers
Pluck in supreme flesh
To smutch supreme littleness.
See the merry limbs in hot Highland fling◊   20
Because some wizard vermin
Charmed from the quiet this revel
When our ears were half lulled
By the dark music
Blown from Sleep's trumpet.   25

1917

Returning, We Hear the Larks

Sombre the night is.
And though we have our lives, we know
What sinister threat lurks there.

Dragging these anguished limbs, we only
   know   5
This poison-blasted track opens on our
    camp –
On a little safe sleep.

But hark! joy – joy – strange joy.
Lo! heights of night ringing with unseen   10
    larks.
Music showering on our upturned list'ning
    faces.

Death could drop from the dark
As easily as song –   15
But song only dropped,
Like a blind man's dreams on the sand
By dangerous tides,
Like a girl's dark hair for she dreams no
   ruin lies there,   20
Or her kisses where a serpent hides.
1917

The Dying Soldier

'Here are houses,' he moaned,
'I could reach but my brain swims.'
Then they thundered and flashed
And shook the earth to its rims.

'They are gunpits,' he gasped,   5
'Our men are at the guns.
Water – water – O water
For one of England's dying sons.'

'We cannot give you water
Were all England in your breath.'   10
'Water – water – O water'
He moaned and swooned to death.
                        1917

Dead Man's Dump

The plunging limbers° over the shattered track
Racketed with their rusty freight,
Stuck out like many crowns of thorns,
And the rusty stakes like sceptres old
To stay the flood of brutish men   5
Upon our brothers dear.

The wheels lurched over sprawled dead
But pained them not, though their bones crunched,
Their shut mouths made no moan.
They lie there huddled, friend and foeman,   10
Man born of man, and born of woman,
And shells go crying over them
From night till night and now.

Earth has waited for them,
All the time of their growth   15
Fretting for their decay:
Now she has them at last!
In the strength of their strength
Suspended – stopped and held.

What fierce imaginings their dark souls lit?   20
Earth! have they gone into you!
Somewhere they must have gone,
And flung on your hard back
Is their soul's sack
Emptied of God-ancestralled essences.   25
Who hurled them out? Who hurled?

None saw their spirits' shadow shake the grass,
Or stood aside for the half used life to pass
Out of those doomed nostrils and the doomed mouth,
When the swift iron burning bee   30
Drained the wild honey of their youth.

What of us who, flung on the shrieking pyre,°
Walk, our usual thoughts untouched,
Our lucky limbs as on ichor° fed,
Immortal seeming ever?   35
Perhaps when the flames beat loud on us,
A fear may choke in our veins
And the startled blood may stop.

The air is loud with death,
The dark air spurts with fire,   40
The explosions ceaseless are.
Timelessly now, some minutes past,
These dead strode time with vigorous life,
Till the shrapnel called 'An end!'
But not to all. In bleeding pangs   45
Some borne on stretchers dreamed of home,
Dear things, war-blotted from their hearts.

Maniac Earth! howling and flying, your bowel
Seared by the jagged fire, the iron love,
The impetuous storm of savage love.   50
Dark Earth! dark Heavens! swinging in chemic smoke,
What dead are born when you kiss each soundless soul
With lightning and thunder from your mined heart,
Which man's self dug, and his blind fingers loosed?

A man's brains splattered on   55
A stretcher-bearer's face;
His shook shoulders slipped their load,
But when they bent to look again
The drowning soul was sunk too deep
For human tenderness.   60

They left this dead with the older dead,
Stretched at the cross roads.

Burnt black by strange decay
Their sinister faces lie,
The lid over each eye,   65
The grass and coloured clay
More motion have than they,
Joined to the great sunk silences.

Here is one not long dead;
His dark hearing caught our far wheels,   70
And the choked soul stretched weak hands
To reach the living word the far wheels said,
The blood-dazed intelligence beating for light,
Crying through the suspense of the far torturing wheels
Swift for the end to break   75
Or the wheels to break,
Cried as the tide of the world broke over his sight.

Will they come? Will they ever come?
Even as the mixed hoofs of the mules,
The quivering-bellied mules,   80
And the rushing wheels all mixed
With his tortured upturned sight.
So we crashed round the bend,
We heard his weak scream,
We heard his very last sound,   85
And our wheels grazed his dead face.

                                1918

SECTION C
Wilfred Owen

SECTION C: Poems by Wilfred Owen

✦

1914

War broke: and now the Winter of the world
With perishing great darkness closes in.
The foul tornado, centred at Berlin,°
Is over all the width of Europe whirled,
Rending the sails of progress. Rent or furled   5
Are all Art's ensigns. Verse wails. Now begin
Famines of thought and feeling. Love's wine's thin.
The grain of human Autumn rots, down-hurled.

For after Spring had bloomed in early Greece,°
And Summer blazed her glory out with Rome,°   10
An Autumn softly fell, a harvest home,
A slow grand age, and rich with all increase.
But now, for us, wild Winter, and the need
Of sowings for new Spring, and blood for seed.
                    drafted 1914; *revised* 1917–1918

Nocturne°

Now, as the warm approach of honied slumber blurs my
          sense,
Before I yield me to th'enchantment of my bed,
God rest all souls in toil and turbulence,
All men a-weary seeking bread;
God rest them all tonight!   5
Let sleep expunge
The day's monotonous vistas from their sight;
And let them plunge
Deep down the dusky firmament of reverie
And drowse of dreams with me.   10

Ah! I should drowse away the night most peacefully
But that there toil too many bodies unreposed
Who fain would fall on lethargy;
Too many leaden eyes unclosed;
And aching hands amove   15
Interminably,
Beneath the light that night will not remove;
Too many brains that rave in dust and steam!
They rave, but cannot dream!

                        1915

Anthem for Doomed Youth

What passing-bells° for these who die as cattle?
   – Only the monstrous anger of the guns.
   Only the stuttering rifles' rapid rattle
Can patter out their hasty orisons.°
No mockeries now for them; no prayers nor bells;   5
   Nor any voice of mourning save the choirs, –
The shrill, demented choirs of wailing shells;
   And bugles calling for them from sad shires.°

What candles may be held to speed them all?
   Not in the hands of boys but in their eyes   10
Shall shine the holy glimmers of goodbyes.
   The pallor of girls' brows shall be their pall;
Their flowers the tenderness of patient minds,
And each slow dusk a drawing-down of blinds.

                        1917

Dulce et Decorum Est◇

Bent double, like old beggars under sacks,
Knock-kneed, coughing like hags, we cursed through sludge,
Till on the haunting flares we turned our backs
And towards our distant rest began to trudge.
Men marched asleep. Many had lost their boots   5
But limped on, blood-shod. All went lame; all blind;
Drunk with fatigue; deaf even to the hoots
Of tired, outstripped Five-Nines◇ that dropped behind.

Gas! GAS! Quick, boys! – An ecstasy of fumbling,
Fitting the clumsy helmets just in time;   10
But someone still was yelling out and stumbling,
And flound'ring like a man in fire or lime …
Dim, through the misty panes and thick green light,
As under a green sea, I saw him drowning.

In all my dreams, before my helpless sight,   15
He plunges at me, guttering, choking, drowning.

If in some smothering dreams you too could pace
Behind the wagon that we flung him in,
And watch the white eyes writhing in his face,
His hanging face, like a devil's sick of sin;   20
If you could hear, at every jolt, the blood
Come gargling from the froth-corrupted lungs,
Obscene as cancer, bitter as the cud
Of vile, incurable sores on innocent tongues, –
My friend,◇ you would not tell with such high zest   25
To children ardent for some desperate glory,
The old Lie: Dulce et decorum est
Pro patria mori.

1917–1918

The Next War

> War's a joke for me and you,
> While we know such dreams are true.
> SIEGFRIED SASSOON

Out there, we walked quite friendly up to Death, –
   Sat down and ate beside him, cool and bland, –
   Pardoned his spilling mess-tins in our hand.
We've sniffed the green thick odour of his breath, –
Our eyes wept, but our courage didn't writhe.   5
   He's spat at us with bullets, and he's coughed
   Shrapnel. We chorused if he sang aloft,
We whistled while he shaved us with his scythe.

Oh, Death was never enemy of ours!
   We laughed at him, we leagued° with him, old chum.   10
No soldier's paid to kick against His powers.
   We laughed, – knowing that better men would come,
And greater wars: when every fighter brags
He fights on Death, for lives; not men, for flags.

1917–1918

The Chances

I 'mind as how the night before that show
Us five got talkin'; we was in the know.
'Ah well,' says Jimmy, and he's seen some scrappin',
'There ain't no more than five things as can happen, –
You get knocked out; else wounded, bad or cushy;   5
Scuppered; or nowt except you're feelin' mushy.'

One of us got the knock-out, blown to chops;
One lad was hurt, like, losin' both his props;
And one – to use the word of hypocrites –
Had the misfortune to be took by Fritz.°   10
Now me, I wasn't scratched, praise God Almighty,
Though next time please I'll thank Him for a blighty.°
But poor old Jim, he's livin' and he's not;
He reckoned he'd five chances, and he had:
He's wounded, killed, and pris'ner, all the lot,   15
The flamin' lot all rolled in one. Jim's mad.
                         1917–1918

The Sentry

We'd found an old Boche° dug-out, and he knew,
And gave us hell; for shell on frantic shell
Lit full on top, but never quite burst through.
Rain, guttering down in waterfalls of slime,
Kept slush waist-high and rising hour by hour,   5
And choked the steps too thick with clay to climb.
What murk of air remained stank old, and sour
With fumes from whizz-bangs, and the smell of men
Who'd lived there years, and left their curse in the den,
If not their corpses …

There we herded from the blast   10
Of whizz-bangs; but one found our door at last, –
Buffeting eyes and breath, snuffing the candles,
And thud! flump! thud! down the steep steps came thumping
And sploshing in the flood, deluging muck,
The sentry's body; then his rifle, handles   15
Of old Boche bombs, and mud in ruck on ruck.
We dredged it up, for dead, until he whined,
'O sir – my eyes, – I'm blind, – I'm blind, – I'm blind.'
Coaxing, I held a flame against his lids
And said if he could see the least blurred light   20
He was not blind; in time they'd get all right.
'I can't,' he sobbed. Eyeballs, huge-bulged like squids',
Watch my dreams still, – yet I forgot him there
In posting Next for duty, and sending a scout
To beg a stretcher somewhere, and flound'ring about   25
To other posts under the shrieking air.

Those other wretches, how they bled and spewed,
And one who would have drowned himself for good, –
I try not to remember these things now.
Let Dread hark back for one word only: how,   30
Half-listening to that sentry's moans and jumps,
And the wild chattering of his shivered teeth,
Renewed most horribly whenever crumps
Pummelled the roof and slogged the air beneath, –
Through the dense din, I say, we heard him shout   35
'I see your lights!' – But ours had long gone out.

1917–1918

Exposure

Our brains ache, in the merciless iced east winds that knive
     us …
Wearied we keep awake because the night is silent …
Low, drooping flares confuse our memory of the salient° …
Worried by silence, sentries whisper, curious, nervous,
     But nothing happens.   5

Watching, we hear the mad gusts tugging on the wire,
Like twitching agonies of men among its brambles.
Northward, incessantly, the flickering gunnery rumbles,
Far off, like a dull rumour of some other war.
     What are we doing here?   10

The poignant misery of dawn begins to grow …
We only know war lasts, rain soaks, and clouds sag stormy.
Dawn massing in the east her melancholy army
Attacks once more in ranks on shivering ranks of grey,
     But nothing happens.   15

Sudden successive flights of bullets streak the silence.
Less deathly than the air that shudders black with snow,
With sidelong flowing flakes that flock, pause, and renew;
We watch them wandering up and down the wind's
     nonchalance,
     But nothing happens.   20

Pale flakes with fingering stealth come feeling for our faces –
We cringe in holes, back on forgotten dreams, and stare,
     snow-dazed,
Deep into grassier ditches. So we drowse, sun-dozed,
Littered with blossoms trickling where the blackbird fusses,
     – Is it that we are dying?   25

Slowly our ghosts drag home: glimpsing the sunk fires,
    glozed[◊]
With crusted dark-red jewels; crickets jingle there;
For hours the innocent mice rejoice: the house is theirs;
Shutters and doors, all closed: on us the doors are closed, –
    We turn back to our dying.   30

Since we believe not otherwise can kind fires burn;
Nor ever suns smile true on child, or field, or fruit.
For God's invincible spring our love is made afraid;
Therefore, not loath, we lie out here; therefore were born,
    For love of God seems dying.   35

Tonight, this frost will fasten on this mud and us,
Shrivelling many hands, puckering foreheads crisp.
The burying-party, picks and shovels in shaking grasp,
Pause over half-known faces. All their eyes are ice,
    But nothing happens.   40

               1917–1918

S.I.W.[◊]

             I will to the King,
And offer him consolation in his trouble,
For that man there has set his teeth to die,
And being one that hates obedience,
Discipline, and orderliness of life,
I cannot mourn him.
W. B. YEATS

I The Prologue
Patting goodbye, doubtless they told the lad
He'd always show the Hun a brave man's face;
Father would sooner him dead than in disgrace, –
Was proud to see him going, aye, and glad.
Perhaps his mother whimpered how she'd fret   5
Until he got a nice safe wound to nurse.

Sisters would wish girls too could shoot, charge, curse …
Brothers – would send his favourite cigarette.
Each week, month after month, they wrote the same,
Thinking him sheltered in some Y. M. Hut,◇   10
Because he said so, writing on his butt
Where once an hour a bullet missed its aim.
And misses teased the hunger of his brain.
His eyes grew old with wincing, and his hand
Reckless with ague. Courage leaked, as sand   15
From the best sandbags after years of rain.
But never leave, wound, fever, trench-foot,◇ shock,
Untrapped◇ the wretch. And death seemed still withheld
For torture of lying machinally shelled,
At the pleasure of this world's Powers who'd run amok.   20

He'd seen men shoot their hands, on night patrol.
Their people never knew. Yet they were vile.
'Death sooner than dishonour, that's the style!'
So Father said.

II The Action

                    One dawn, our wire patrol
Carried him. This time, Death had not missed.   25
We could do nothing but wipe his bleeding cough.
Could it be accident? – Rifles go off …
Not sniped? No. (Later they found the English ball.◇)

III The Poem

It was the reasoned crisis of his soul
Against more days of inescapable thrall,◇   30
Against infrangibly◇ wired and blind trench wall
Curtained with fire, roofed in with creeping fire,
Slow grazing fire, that would not burn him whole
But kept him for death's promises and scoff,
And life's half-promising, and both their riling.   35

IV The Epilogue

With him they buried the muzzle his teeth had kissed,
And truthfully wrote the mother, 'Tim died smiling.'
                                        1917–1918

The Send-Off

Down the close darkening lanes they sang their way
To the siding-shed,
And lined the train with faces grimly gay.

Their breasts were stuck all white with wreath and spray
As men's are, dead.   5

Dull porters watched them, and a casual tramp
Stood staring hard,
Sorry to miss them from the upland camp.°

Then, unmoved, signals nodded, and a lamp
Winked to the guard.   10

So secretly, like wrongs hushed-up, they went.
They were not ours:
We never heard to which front these were sent;

Nor there if they yet mock what women meant
Who gave them flowers.   15

Shall they return to beating of great bells°
In wild train-loads?
A few, a few, too few for drums and yells,

May creep back, silent, to village wells,
Up half-known roads.   20

1918

Futility

Move him into the sun –
Gently its touch awoke him once,
At home, whispering of fields half-sown.
Always it woke him, even in France,
Until this morning and this snow.   5
If anything might rouse him now
The kind old sun will know.

Think how it wakes the seeds –
Woke once the clays of a cold star.°
Are limbs, so dear achieved, are sides   10
Full-nerved, still warm, too hard to stir?
Was it for this the clay grew tall?
– O what made fatuous sunbeams toil
To break earth's sleep at all?

                                    1918

Strange Meeting

It seemed that out of battle I escaped
Down some profound dull tunnel, long since scooped
Through granites which titanic° wars had groined.

Yet also there encumbered sleepers groaned,
Too fast in thought or death to be bestirred.   5
Then, as I probed them, one sprang up, and stared
With piteous recognition in fixed eyes,
Lifting distressful hands, as if to bless.
And by his smile, I knew that sullen hall, –
By his dead smile I knew we stood in Hell.   10

With a thousand pains that vision's face was grained;
Yet no blood reached there from the upper ground,
And no guns thumped, or down the flues° made moan.
'Strange friend,' I said, 'here is no cause to mourn.'
'None,' said that other, 'save the undone years,   15
The hopelessness. Whatever hope is yours,
Was my life also; I went hunting wild
After the wildest beauty in the world,
Which lies not calm in eyes, or braided hair,
But mocks the steady running of the hour,   20
And if it grieves, grieves richlier than here.
For by my glee might many men have laughed,
And of my weeping something had been left,
Which must die now. I mean the truth untold,
The pity of war, the pity war distilled.   25
Now men will go content with what we spoiled,
Or, discontent, boil bloody, and be spilled.
They will be swift with swiftness of the tigress.
None will break ranks, though nations trek from progress.
Courage was mine, and I had mystery,   30
Wisdom was mine, and I had mastery:
To miss the march of this retreating world
Into vain citadels that are not walled.
Then, when much blood had clogged their chariot-wheels,
I would go up and wash them from sweet wells,   35
Even with truths that lie too deep for taint.
I would have poured my spirit without stint
But not through wounds; not on the cess of war.
Foreheads of men have bled where no wounds were.

'I am the enemy you killed, my friend.   40
I knew you in this dark: for so you frowned
Yesterday through me as you jabbed and killed.
I parried; but my hands were loath and cold.
Let us sleep now....'
                                            1918

49

Smile, Smile, Smile⋄

Head to limp head, the sunk-eyed wounded scanned
Yesterday's *Mail*;⋄ the casualties (typed small)
And (large) Vast Booty from our Latest Haul.⋄
Also, they read of Cheap Homes, not yet planned,
'For,' said the paper, 'when this war is done   5
The men's first instincts will be making homes.
Meanwhile their foremost need is aerodromes,
It being certain war has but begun.
Peace would do wrong to our undying dead, –
The sons we offered might regret they died   10
If we got nothing lasting in their stead.
We must be solidly indemnified.
Though all be worthy Victory which all bought,
We rulers sitting in this ancient spot
Would wrong our very selves if we forgot   15
The greatest glory will be theirs who fought,
Who kept this nation in integrity.'
Nation? – The half-limbed readers did not chafe
But smiled at one another curiously
Like secret men who know their secret safe.   20
(This is the thing they know and never speak,
That England⋄ one by one had fled to France,
Not many elsewhere now, save under France.)
Pictures of these broad smiles appear each week,
And people in whose voice real feeling rings   25
Say: How they smile! They're happy now, poor things.
                                        1918

Spring Offensive

Halted against the shade of a last hill
They fed, and eased of pack-loads, were at ease;
And leaning on the nearest chest or knees
Carelessly slept.
    But many there stood still
To face the stark blank sky beyond the ridge,   5
Knowing their feet had come to the end of the world.
Marvelling they stood, and watched the long grass swirled
By the May breeze, murmurous with wasp and midge;
And though the summer oozed into their veins
Like an injected drug for their bodies' pains,   10
Sharp on their souls hung the imminent ridge of grass,
Fearfully flashed the sky's mysterious glass.

Hour after hour they ponder the warm field
And the far valley behind, where buttercups
Had blessed with gold their slow boots coming up;   15
When even the little brambles would not yield
But clutched and clung to them like sorrowing arms.
They breathe like trees unstirred.

Till like a cold gust thrills the little word
At which each body and its soul begird°   20
And tighten them for battle. No alarms
Of bugles, no high flags, no clamorous haste, –
Only a lift and flare of eyes that faced
The sun, like a friend with whom their love is done.
O larger shone that smile against the sun, –   25
Mightier than his whose bounty these have spurned.

So, soon they topped the hill, and raced together
Over an open stretch of herb and heather
Exposed. And instantly the whole sky burned
With fury against them; earth set sudden cups   30
In thousands for their blood; and the green slope
Chasmed and deepened sheer to infinite space.

Of them who running on that last high place
Breasted the surf of bullets, or went up
On the hot blast and fury of hell's upsurge,   35
Or plunged and fell away past this world's verge,
Some say God caught them even before they fell.

But what say such as from existence' brink
Ventured but drave° too swift to sink,
The few who rushed in the body to enter hell,   40
And there out-fiending all its fiends and flames
With superhuman inhumanities,
Long-famous glories, immemorial shames –
And crawling slowly back, have by degrees
Regained cool peaceful air in wonder –   45
Why speak not they of comrades that went under?
                                        1918

SECTION D
Siegfried Sassoon

SECTION D: Poems by Siegfried Sassoon

✦

A Letter Home
(To Robert Graves)

I

Here I'm sitting in the gloom
Of my quiet attic room.
France goes rolling all around,
Fledged with forest May has crowned.
And I puff my pipe, calm-hearted,   5
Thinking how the fighting started,
Wondering when we'll ever end it,
Back to Hell with Kaiser send it,
Gag the noise, pack up and go,
Clockwork soldiers in a row.   10
I've got better things to do
Than to waste my time on you.

II

Robert, when I drowse to-night,
Skirting lawns of sleep to chase
Shifting dreams in mazy light,   15
Somewhere then I'll see your face
Turning back to bid me follow
Where I wag my arms and hollo,
Over hedges hasting after
Crooked smile and baffling laughter,   20
Running tireless, floating, leaping,
Down your web-hung woods and valleys,
Garden glooms and hornbeam alleys,
Where the glowworm stars are peeping,
Till I find you, quiet as stone   25
On a hill-top all alone,

Staring outward, gravely pondering
Jumbled leagues of hillock-wandering.

III

You and I have walked together
In the starving winter weather.   30
We've been glad because we knew
Time's too short and friends are few.
We've been sad because we missed
One whose yellow head was kissed
By the gods, who thought about him   35
Till they couldn't do without him.
Now he's here again; I've seen
Soldier David dressed in green,
Standing in a wood that swings
To the madrigal he sings.   40
He's come back, all mirth and glory,
Like the prince in a fairy story.
Winter called him far away;
Blossoms bring him home with May.

IV

Well, I know you'll swear it's true   45
That you found him decked in blue
Striding up through morning-land
With a cloud on either hand.
Out in Wales, you'll say, he marches
Arm-in-arm with oaks and larches;   50
Hides all night in hilly nooks,
Laughs at dawn in tumbling brooks.
Yet, it's certain, here he teaches
Outpost-schemes to groups of beeches.
And I'm sure, as here I stand,   55
That he shines through every land,
That he sings in every place
Where we're thinking of his face.

V

Robert, there's a war in France;
Everywhere men bang and blunder,   60
Sweat and swear and worship Chance,
Creep and blink through cannon thunder.
Rifles crack and bullets flick,
Sing and hum like hornet-swarms.
Bones are smashed and buried quick.   65
Yet, through stunning battle storms,
All the while I watch the spark
Lit to guide me; for I know
Dreams will triumph, though the dark
Scowls above me where I go.   70
You can hear me; *you* can mingle
Radiant folly with my jingle.
War's a joke for me and you
While we know such dreams are true!
                              1916

The Hero

'Jack fell as he'd have wished,' the Mother said,
And folded up the letter that she'd read.
'The Colonel writes so nicely.' Something broke
In the tired voice that quavered to a choke.
She half looked up. 'We mothers are so proud   5
Of our dead soldiers.' Then her face was bowed.

Quietly the Brother Officer went out.
He'd told the poor old dear some gallant lies
That she would nourish all her days, no doubt.
For while he coughed and mumbled, her weak eyes   10
Had shone with gentle triumph, brimmed with joy,
Because he'd been so brave, her glorious boy.

He thought how 'Jack', cold-footed, useless swine,
Had panicked down the trench that night the mine
Went up at Wicked Corner;° how he'd tried   15
To get sent home, and how, at last, he died,
Blown to small bits. And no one seemed to care
Except that lonely woman with white hair.

published 1917

A Working Party

Three hours ago he blundered up the trench,
Sliding and poising, groping with his boots;
Sometimes he tripped and lurched against the walls
With hands that pawed the sodden bags of chalk.
He couldn't see the man who walked in front;   5
Only he heard the drum and rattle of feet
Stepping along barred trench boards, often splashing
Wretchedly where the sludge was ankle-deep.

Voices would grunt 'Keep to your right – make way!'
When squeezing past some men from the front-line: 10
White faces peered, puffing a point of red;
Candles and braziers glinted through the chinks
And curtain-flaps of dug-outs; then the gloom
Swallowed his sense of sight; he stooped and swore
Because a sagging wire had caught his neck.   15

A flare went up; the shining whiteness spread
And flickered upward, showing nimble rats
And mounds of glimmering sand-bags, bleached with rain;
Then the slow silver moment died in dark.
The wind came posting by with chilly gusts   20
And buffeting at corners, piping thin.
And dreary through the crannies; rifle-shots
Would split and crack and sing along the night,
And shells came calmly through the drizzling air
To burst with hollow bang below the hill.   25

published 1917

The General

'Good-morning; good-morning!' the General said
When we met him last week on our way to the line.
Now the soldiers he smiled at are most of 'em dead,
And we're cursing his staff for incompetent swine.
'He's a cheery old card,' grunted Harry to Jack   5
As they slogged up to Arras° with rifle and pack.

     .   .   .   .

But he did for them both by his plan of attack.
> *published* 1918

Base Details

If I were fierce, and bald, and short of breath,
    I'd live with scarlet Majors at the Base,
And speed glum heroes up the line to death.
    You'd see me with my puffy petulant face,
Guzzling and gulping in the best hotel,   5
    Reading the Roll of Honour.° 'Poor young chap,'
I'd say – 'I used to know his father well;
    Yes, we've lost heavily in this last scrap.'
And when the war is done and youth stone dead,
I'd toddle safely home and die – in bed.   10
> *published* 1918

Song-Books of the War

In fifty years, when peace outshines
Remembrance of the battle lines,
Adventurous lads will sigh and cast
Proud looks upon the plundered past.
On summer morn or winter's night,   5
Their hearts will kindle for the fight,
Reading a snatch of soldier-song,
Savage and jaunty, fierce and strong;
And through the angry marching rhymes
Of blind regret and haggard mirth,   10
They'll envy us the dazzling times
When sacrifice absolved our earth.

Some ancient man with silver locks
Will lift his weary face to say:
'War was a fiend who stopped our clocks   15
Although we met him grim and gay.'
And then he'll speak of Haig's° last drive,
Marvelling that any came alive
Out of the shambles that men built
And smashed, to cleanse the world of guilt.   20
But the boys, with grin and sidelong glance,
Will think, 'Poor grandad's day is done.'
And dream of lads who fought in France
And lived in time to share the fun.

published 1918

Suicide in the Trenches

I knew a simple soldier boy
Who grinned at life in empty joy,
Slept soundly through the lonesome dark,
And whistled early with the lark.

In winter trenches, cowed and glum,   5
With crumps and lice and lack of rum,
He put a bullet through his brain.
No one spoke of him again.

       .   .   .   .

You smug-faced crowds with kindling eye
Who cheer when soldier lads march by,   10
Sneak home and pray you'll never know
The hell where youth and laughter go.

published 1918

The Dug-Out

Why do you lie with your legs ungainly huddled,
And one arm bent across your sullen, cold,
Exhausted face? It hurts my heart to watch you,
Deep-shadow'd from the candle's guttering gold;
And you wonder why I shake you by the shoulder;   5
Drowsy, you mumble and sigh and turn your head …
You are too young to fall asleep for ever;
And when you sleep you remind me of the dead.

1918

Counter-Attack

We'd gained our first objective hours before
While dawn broke like a face with blinking eyes,
Pallid, unshaved and thirsty, blind with smoke.
Things seemed all right at first. We held their line,
With bombers posted, Lewis guns° well placed,   5
And clink of shovels deepening the shallow trench.
    The place was rotten with dead; green clumsy legs
    High-booted, sprawled and grovelled along the saps
    And trunks, face downward, in the sucking mud,
    Wallowed like trodden sand-bags loosely filled;   10
    And naked sodden buttocks, mats of hair,
    Bulged, clotted heads slept in the plastering slime.
    And then the rain began, – the jolly old rain!

A yawning soldier knelt against the bank,
Staring across the morning blear with fog;   15
He wondered when the Allemands° would get busy;
And then, of course, they started with five-nines
Traversing, sure as fate, and never a dud.
Mute in the clamour of shells he watched them burst
Spouting dark earth and wire with gusts from hell,   20
While posturing giants dissolved in drifts of smoke.
He crouched and flinched, dizzy with galloping fear,
Sick for escape, – loathing the strangled horror
And butchered, frantic gestures of the dead.

An officer came blundering down the trench: 25
'Stand-to and man the fire-step!'° On he went …
Gasping and bawling, 'Fire-step … counter-attack!'
    Then the haze lifted. Bombing on the right
    Down the old sap: machine-guns on the left;
    And stumbling figures looming out in front.   30
    'O Christ, they're coming at us!' Bullets spat,

And he remembered his rifle ... rapid fire ...
And started blazing wildly ... then a bang
Crumpled and spun him sideways, knocked him out
To grunt and wriggle: none heeded him; he choked   35
And fought the flapping veils of smothering gloom,
Lost in a blurred confusion of yells and groans ...
Down, and down, and down, he sank and drowned,
Bleeding to death. The counter-attack had failed.

published 1918

Glory of Women

You love us when we're heroes, home on leave,
Or wounded in a mentionable place.
You worship decorations; you believe
That chivalry redeems the war's disgrace.
You make us shells.° You listen with delight,   5
By tales of dirt and danger fondly thrilled.
You crown our distant ardours while we fight,
And mourn our laurelled° memories when we're killed.
You can't believe that British troops 'retire'
When hell's last horror breaks them, and they run,   10
Trampling the terrible corpses – blind with blood.
   O German mother dreaming by the fire,
    While you are knitting socks to send your son
    His face is trodden deeper in the mud.

published 1918

Sick Leave

When I'm asleep, dreaming and lulled and warm, –
They come, the homeless ones, the noiseless dead.
While the dim charging breakers of the storm
Bellow and drone and rumble overhead,
Out of the gloom they gather about my bed.   5
    They whisper to my heart; their thoughts are mine.
    'Why are you here with all your watches ended?
    From Ypres to Frise we sought you in the Line.'
In bitter safety I awake, unfriended;
And while the dawn begins with slashing rain   10
I think of the Battalion in the mud.
'When are you going out to them again?
Are they not still your brothers through our blood?'
                    published 1918

Aftermath

Have you forgotten yet? …
For the world's events have rumbled on since those gagged
    days,
Like traffic checked while at the crossing of city-ways:
And the haunted gap in your mind has filled with thoughts
    that flow
Like clouds in the lit heaven of life; and you're a man
    reprieved to go,   5
Taking your peaceful share of Time, with joy to spare.
But the past is just the same – and War's a bloody game …
Have you forgotten yet? …
Look down, and swear by the slain of the War that you'll
    never forget.

Do you remember the dark months you held the sector at
    Mametz° –   10
The nights you watched and wired and dug and piled
    sandbags on parapets ?
Do you remember the rats; and the stench
Of corpses rotting in front of the front-line trench –
And dawn coming, dirty-white, and chill with a hopeless
    rain?
Do you ever stop and ask, 'Is it all going to happen again?'   15

Do you remember that hour of din before the attack –
And the anger, the blind compassion that seized and shook
    you then
As you peered at the doomed and haggard faces of your men?
Do you remember the stretcher-cases lurching back
With dying eyes and lolling heads – those ashen-grey   20
Masks of the lads who once were keen and kind and gay?

Have you forgotten yet? …
Look up, and swear by the green of the spring that you'll
    never forget.

1919

Everyone Sang

Everyone suddenly burst out singing;
And I was filled with such delight
As prisoned birds must find in freedom,
Winging wildly across the white
Orchards and dark-green fields; on – on – and out of sight.   5

Everyone's voice was suddenly lifted;
And beauty came like the setting sun:
My heart was shaken with tears; and horror
Drifted away ... O, but Everyone
Was a bird; and the song was wordless; the singing will
    never be done.   10

           1919

To One Who Was With Me in the War

It was too long ago – that Company which we served with ...
We call it back in visual fragments, you and I,
Who seem, ourselves, like relics casually preserved with
Our mindfulness of old bombardments when the sky
With blundering din blinked cavernous.   5
           Yet a sense of power
Invades us when, recapturing an ungodly hour
Of ante-zero crisis, in one thought we've met
To stand in some redoubt° of Time, – to share again
All but the actual wetness of the flare-lit rain,   10
All but the living presences who haunt us yet
With gloom-patrolling eyes.
           Remembering, we forget
Much that was monstrous, much that clogged our souls with
    clay

When hours were guides who led us by the longest way –   15
And when the worst had been endured could still disclose
Another worst to thwart us …
                            We forget our fear …
And, while the uncouth Event begins to lour less near,
Discern the mad magnificence whose storm-light throws   20
Wild shadows on these after-thoughts that send your brain
Back beyond Peace, exploring sunken ruinous roads.
Your brain, with files of flitting forms hump-backed with
          loads,
On its own helmet hears the tinkling drops of rain, –
Follows to an end some night-relief, and strangely sees   25
The quiet no-man's-land of daybreak, jagg'd with trees
That loom like giant Germans …
                            I'll go with you, then,
Since you must play this game of ghosts. At listening-posts
We'll peer across dim craters; joke with jaded men   30
Whose names we've long forgotten. (Stoop low there; it's the
          place
The sniper enfilades.°) Round the next bay you'll meet
A drenched platoon-commander; chilled, he drums his feet
On squelching duck-boards; winds his wrist-watch; turns his
          head,
And shows you how you looked, – your ten-years-vanished
          face,   35
Hoping the War will end next week. …
                            What's that you said?
                                        published 1927

On Passing the New Menin Gate

Who will remember, passing through this Gate,°
The unheroic Dead who fed the guns?
Who shall absolve the foulness of their fate, –
Those doomed, conscripted, unvictorious ones?
    Crudely renewed, the Salient holds its own.   5
    Paid are its dim defenders by this pomp;
    Paid, with a pile of peace-complacent stone,
    The armies who endured that sullen swamp.

Here was the world's worst wound. And here with pride
'Their name liveth for ever,' the Gateway claims.   10
Was ever an immolation so belied
As these intolerably nameless names?
Well might the Dead who struggled in the slime
Rise and deride this sepulchre of crime.

published 1927

SECTION E
Edmund Blunden

SECTION E: Poems by Edmund Blunden

◆

Festubert:° the Old German Line

Sparse mists of moonlight hurt our eyes
    With gouged and scourged uncertainties
    Of soul and soil in agonies

One derelict grim skeleton
That drench and dry had battened on   5
Still seemed to wish us malison;°

Still zipped across the gouts of lead
Or cracked like whipcracks overhead;
The gray rags fluttered on the dead.
              1916

The Unchangeable

Though I within these two last years of grace
Have seen bright Ancre° scourged to brackish mire,
And meagre Belgian becks° by dale and chace
Stamped into sloughs of death with battering fire –
Spite of all this, I sing you high and low,   5
My old loves, Waters, be you shoal or deep,
Waters whose lazy continual flow
Learns at the drizzling weir the tongue of sleep.
For Sussex cries from primrose lags and brakes,
'Why do you leave my woods untrod so long?   10
Still float the bronze carp on my lilied lakes,
Still the wood-fairies round my spring wells throng;
And chancing lights on willowy waterbreaks
Dance to the bubbling brooks of elfin song.'
              1917

Les Halles d'Ypres◇

A tangle of iron rods and spluttered beams,
    On brickwork past the skill of a mason to mend:
A wall with a bright blue poster – odd as dreams
    Is the city's latter end.

A shapeless obelisk looms Saint Martin's spire,◇   5
    Now a lean aiming-mark for the German guns;
And the Cloth Hall◇ crouches beside, disfigured with fire,
    The glory of Flanders once.

Only the foursquare tower still bears the trace
    Of beauty that was, and strong embattled age,   10
And gilded ceremonies and pride of place –
    Before this senseless rage.

And still you may see (below the noon serene,
    The mysterious, changeless vault of sharp blue light),
The pigeons come to the tower, and flaunt and preen,   15
    And flicker in playful flight.

                                 1917

Reunion in War

The windmill in his smock of white
    Stared from his little crest,
Like a slow smoke was the moonlight
    As I went like one possessed

Where the glebe path makes shortest way;   5
    The stammering wicket swung.
I passed amid the crosses grey
    Where opiate yew-boughs hung.

The bleached grass shuddered into sighs,
    The dogs that knew this moon   10
Far up were hurrying sheep, the cries
    Of hunting owls went on.

And I among the dead made haste
    And over flat vault stones
Set in the path unheeding paced   15
    Nor thought of those chill bones.

Thus to my sweetheart's cottage I,
    Who long had been away,
Turned as the traveller turns adry
    To brooks to moist his clay.   20

Her cottage stood like a dream, so clear
    And yet so dark; and now
I thought to find my more than dear
    And if she'd kept her vow.

Old house-dog from his barrel came   25
    Without a voice, and knew
And licked my hand; all seemed the same
    To the moonlight and the dew.

By the white damson then I took
    The tallest osier wand   30
And thrice upon her casement strook,
    And she, so fair, so fond,

Looked out, and saw in wild delight,
    And tiptoed down to me,
And cried in silent joy that night   35
    Beside the bullace tree.

O cruel time to take away,
    Or worse to bring agen;
Why slept not I in Flanders clay
    With all the murdered men?   40

For I had changed, or she had changed,
  Though true love both had been,
Even while we kissed we stood estranged
  With the ghosts of war between.

We had not met but a moment ere   45
  War baffled joy, and cried,
'Love's but a madness, a burnt flare;
  The shell's a madman's bride.'

The cottage stood, poor stone and wood,
  Poorer than stone stood I;   50
Then from her kind arms moved in a mood
  As grey as the cereclothed sky.

The roosts were stirred, each little bird
  Called fearfully out for day;
The church clock with his dead voice whirred 55
  As if he bade me stay

To trace with foolish fingers all
  The letters on the stones
Where thick beneath the twitch roots crawl
  In dead men's envied bones.   60

                    published 1922

The Sentry's Mistake

The chapel at the crossways bore no scar,
Nor near had whining covey of shells yet pounced,
The calm saints in the chapel knew no war,
No meaning there the horizon's roars announced;
    We halted, and were glad; the country lay   5
    After our marching like a sabbath day.

Round the still quadrangle of the great farm
The company soon had settled their new home;
The cherry-boughs were beckoning every arm,
The stream ran wrinkling by with playful foam,   10
    And when the guard was at the gateway set,
    Surrounding pastoral sweetly stole their wit.

So out upon the road, gamekeeper-like,
The cowman now turned warrior measured out
His up-and-down sans cursed bundook and spike,°   15
Under his arm a cudgel brown and stout;
    An air of comfort and kind ownership,
    A philosophic smile upon his lip.

For it seemed sin to soil the harmonious air
With the parade of weapons built to kill.   20
But now a flagged car came ill-omened there.
The crimson-mottled monarch, shocked and shrill,
    Sent our poor sentry scampering for his gun,
    Made him once more 'the terror of the Hun'.
                        published 1928

The Zonnebeke Road◊

Morning, if this late withered light can claim
Some kindred with that merry flame
Which the young day was wont to fling through space!
Agony stares from each gray face.
And yet the day is come; stand down! stand down!   5
Your hands unclasp from rifles while you can,
The frost has pierced them to the bended bone?
Why, see old Stevens there, that iron man,
Melting the ice to shave his grotesque chin:
Go ask him, shall we win?   10
I never liked this bay, some foolish fear
Caught me the first time that I came in here;
That dugout fallen in awakes, perhaps,
Some formless haunting of some corpse's chaps.
True, and wherever we have held the line,   15
There were such corners, seeming-saturnine◊
    For no good cause.
                        Now where Haymarket◊ starts,
That is no place for soldiers with weak hearts;
The minenwerfers◊ have it to the inch.
Look, how the snowdust whisks along the road,   20
Piteous and silly; the stones themselves must flinch
In this east wind; the low sky like a load
Hangs over – a dead-weight. But what a pain
Must gnaw where its clay cheek
Crushes the shell-chopped trees that fang the plain –   25
The ice-bound throat gulps out a gargoyle◊ shriek.
The wretched wire before the village line
Rattles like rusty brambles or dead bine,◊
And then the daylight oozes into dun;
Black pillars, those are trees where roadways run.   30

Even Ypres now would warm our souls; fond fool,
Our tour's but one night old, seven more to cool!
O screaming dumbness, O dull clashing death,
Shreds of dead grass and willows, homes and men,
Watch as you will, men clench their chattering teeth   35
And freeze you back with that one hope, disdain.

published 1928

Concert Party: Busseboom[◊]

The stage was set, the house was packed,
    The famous troop began;
Our laughter thundered, act by act;
    Time light as sunbeams ran.

Dance sprang and spun and neared and fled,   5
    Jest chirped at gayest pitch,
Rhythm dazzled, action sped
    Most comically rich.

With generals and lame privates both
    Such charms worked wonders, till   10
The show was over – lagging loth
    We faced the sunset chill;

And standing on the sandy way,
    With the cracked church peering past,
We heard another matinée,   15
    We heard the maniac blast

Of barrage south by Saint Eloi,[◊]
    And the red lights flaming there
Called madness: Come, my bonny boy,
    And dance to the latest air.   20

To this new concert, white we stood;
    Cold certainty held our breath;
While men in the tunnels below Larch Wood[◦]
    Were kicking men to death.

                1917

Vlamertinghe: ◦ *Passing the Château, July 1917*

'And all her silken flanks with garlands drest' –
But we are coming to the sacrifice.
Must those have flowers who are not yet gone West?
May those have flowers who live with death and lice?
This must be the floweriest place   5
That earth allows; the queenly face
Of the proud mansion borrows grace for grace
Spite of those brute guns lowing at the skies.

Bold great daisies, golden lights,
Bubbling roses' pinks and whites –   10
Such a gay carpet! poppies by the million;
Such damask! such vermilion!
But if you ask me, mate, the choice of colour
Is scarcely right; this red should have been much duller.

         published 1928

Report on Experience

I have been young, and now am not too old;
And I have seen the righteous forsaken,
His health, his honour and his quality taken.
    This is not what we were formerly told.

I have seen a green country, useful to the race,   5
Knocked silly with guns and mines, its villages vanished,
Even the last rat and last kestrel banished –
    God bless us all, this was peculiar grace.

I knew Seraphina; Nature gave her hue,
Glance, sympathy, note, like one from Eden.   10
I saw her smile warp, heard her lyric deaden;
    She turned to harlotry; – this I took to be new.

Say what you will, our God sees how they run.
These disillusions are His curious proving
That He loves humanity and will go on loving;   15
    Over there are faith, life, virtue in the sun.
                  published 1929

Illusions

Trenches in the moonlight, in the lulling moonlight
Have had their loveliness; when dancing dewy grasses
Caressed us passing along their earthly lanes;
When the crucifix hanging over was strangely illumined,
And one imagined music, one even heard the brave bird   5
In the sighing orchards flute above the weedy well.
There are such moments; forgive me that I note them,
Nor gloze that there comes soon the nemesis of beauty,

In the fluttering relics that at first glimmer wakened
Terror – the no-man's ditch suddenly forking: 10
There, the enemy's best with bombs and brains and courage!
– Softly, swiftly, at once be animal and angel –
But O no, no, they're Death's malkins° dangling in the wire
    For the moon's interpretation.

published 1928

The Ancre at Hamel: Afterwards

Where tongues were loud and hearts were light
    I heard the Ancre flow;
Waking oft at the mid of night
    I heard the Ancre flow.
I heard it crying, that sad rill,   5
    Below the painful ridge,
By the burnt unraftered mill
    And the relic of a bridge.

And could this sighing water seem
    To call me far away,   10
And its pale word dismiss as dream
    The voices of to-day?
The voices in the bright room chilled
    And that mourned on alone,
The silence of the full moon filled   15
    With that brook's troubling tone.

The struggling Ancre had no part
    In these new hours of mine,
And yet its stream ran through my heart,
    I heard it grieve and pine,   20
As if its rainy tortured blood
    Had swirled into my own,
When by its battered bank I stood
    And shared its wounded moan.

published 1928

Third Ypres

Triumph! How strange, how strong had triumph come
On weary hate of foul and endless war
When from its grey gravecloths awoke anew
The summer day. Among the tumbled wreck
Of fascined◇ lines and mounds the light was peering,   5
Half-smiling upon us, and our newfound pride;
The terror of the waiting night outlived,
The time too crowded for the heart to count
All the sharp cost in friends killed on the assault.
No hook of all the octopus had held us,   10
Here stood we trampling down the ancient tyrant.
So shouting dug we among the monstrous pits.

Amazing quiet fell upon the waste,
Quiet intolerable to those who felt
The hurrying batteries beyond the masking hills   15
For their new parley setting themselves in array
In crafty forms unmapped.
                    No, these, smiled faith,
Are dumb for the reason of their overthrow.
They moved not back, they lie among the crews
Twisted and choked, they'll never speak again.   20
Only the copse where once might stand a shrine
Still clacked and suddenly hissed its bullets by.
The War would end, the Line was on the move,
And at a bound the impassable was passed.
We lay and waited with extravagant joy.   25

Now dulls the day and chills; comes there no word
From those who swept through our new lines to flood
The lines beyond? but little comes, and so
Sure as a runner time himself's accosted.
And the slow moments shake their heavy heads,   30

And croak, 'They're done, they'll none of them get through,
They're done, they've all died on the entanglements,
The wire stood up like an unplashed hedge◇ and thorned
With giant spikes – and there they've paid the bill.'

Then comes the black assurance, then the sky's   35
Mute misery lapses into trickling rain,
That wreathes and swims and soon shuts in our world.
And those distorted guns, that lay past use,
Why – miracles not over! – all a-firing!
The rain's no cloak from their sharp eyes. And you,   40
Poor signaller, you I passed by this emplacement,
You whom I warned, poor daredevil, waving your flags,
Amid this screeching I pass you again and shudder
At the lean green flies upon the red flash madding.
Runner, stand by a second. Your message. – He's gone,   45
Falls on a knee, and his right hand uplifted
Claws his last message from his ghostly enemy,
Turns stone-like. Well I liked him, that young runner,
But there's no time for that. O now for the word
To order us flash from these drowning roaring traps   50
And even hurl upon that snarling wire?
Why are our guns so impotent?
                              The grey rain,
Steady as the sand in an hourglass on this day,
Where through the window the red lilac looks,
And all's so still, the chair's odd click is noise –   55
The rain is all heaven's answer, and with hearts
Past reckoning we are carried into night
And even sleep is nodding here and there.
The second night steals through the shrouding rain.
We in our numb thought crouching long have lost   60
The mockery triumph, and in every runner
Have urged the mind's eye see the triumph to come,
The sweet relief, the straggling out of hell
Into whatever burrows may be given
For life's recall. Then the fierce destiny speaks.   65

This was the calm, we shall look back for this.
The hour is come; come, move to the relief!
Dizzy we pass the mule-strewn track where once
The ploughman whistled as he loosed his team;
And where he turned home-hungry on the road,   70
The leaning pollard° marks us hungrier turning,
We crawl to save the remnant who have torn
Back from the tentacled wire, those whom no shell
Has charred into black carcasses – Relief!
They grate their teeth until we take their room,   75
And through the churn of moonless night and mud
And flaming burst and sour gas we are huddled
Into the ditches where they bawl sense awake
And in a frenzy that none could reason calm,
(Whimpering some, and calling on the dead)   80
They turn away: as in a dream they find
Strength in their feet to bear back that strange whim
Their body.
            At the noon of the dreadful day
Our trench and death's is on a sudden stormed
With huge and shattering salvoes, the clay dances   85
In founts of clods around the concrete sties,
Where still the brain devises some last armour
To live out the poor limbs.
                 This wrath's oncoming
Found four of us together in a pillbox,
Skirting the abyss of madness with light phrases,   90
White and blinking, in false smiles grimacing.
The demon grins to see the game, a moment
Passes, and – still the drum-tap dongs my brain
To a whirring void – through the great breach above me
The light comes in with icy shock and the rain   95
Horridly drops. Doctor, talk, talk! if dead
Or stunned I know not; the stinking powdered concrete,
The lyddite° turns me sick – my hair's all full
Of this smashed concrete. O I'll drag you, friends,
Out of the sepulchre into the light of day,   100

For this is day, the pure and sacred day.
And while I squeak and gibber over you,
Look, from the wreck a score of field-mice nimble,
And tame and curious look about them; (these
Calmed me, on these depended my salvation).   105
There comes my sergeant, and by all the powers
The wire is holding to the right battalion,
And I can speak – but I myself first spoken
Hear a known voice now measured even to madness
Call me by name.
               'For God's sake send and help us,   110
Here in a gunpit, all headquarters done for,
Forty or more, the nine-inch came right through,
All splashed with arms and legs, and I myself
The only one not killed not even wounded.
You'll send – God bless you!' The more monstrous fate   115
Shadows our own, the mind swoons doubly burdened,
Taught how for miles our anguish groans and bleeds,
A whole sweet countryside amuck with murder;
Each moment puffed into a year with death.
Still swept the rain, roared guns,   120
Still swooped into the swamps of flesh and blood,
All to the drabness of uncreation sunk,
And all thought dwindled to a moan, Relieve!
But who with what command can now relieve
The dead men from that chaos, or my soul?   125
published 1922

Premature Rejoicing

What's that over there?
                       Thiepval Wood.°
Take a steady look at it; it'll do you good.
Here, these glasses will help you. See any flowers?
There sleeps Titania° (correct – the Wood is ours);   5
There sleeps Titania in a deep dugout,
Waking, she wonders what all the din's about,
And smiles through her tears, and looks ahead ten years,
And sees her Wood again, and her usual Grenadiers,
   All in green,   10
   Music in the moon;
  The burnt rubbish you've just seen
  Won't beat the Fairy Queen;
   All the same, it's a shade too soon
   For you to scribble rhymes   15
   In your army book
   About those times;
   Take another look;
  That's where the difficulty is, over there.
                           published 1930

'Can You Remember?'

Yes, I still remember
    The whole thing in a way;
Edge and exactitude
    Depend on the day.

Of all that prodigious scene 5
    There seems scanty loss,
Though mists mainly float and screen
    Canal, spire and fosse;

Though commonly I fail to name
    That once obvious Hill, 10
And where we went and whence we came
    To be killed, or kill.

Those mists are spiritual
    And luminous-obscure,
Evolved of countless circumstance 15
    Of which I am sure;

Of which, at the instance
    Of sound, smell, change and stir,
New-old shapes for ever
    Intensely recur. 20

And some are sparkling, laughing, singing,
    Young, heroic, mild;
And some incurable, twisted,
    Shrieking, dumb, defiled.
               published 1937

To W. O.⋄ and his Kind

If even you, so able and so keen,
And master of the business you reported
Seem now almost as though you had never been,
And in your simple purpose nearly thwarted,
What hope is there? What harvest from those hours   5
Deliberately, and in the name of truth,
Endured by you? Your witness moves no Powers,
And younger youth resents your sentient youth.

You would have stayed me with some parable,
The grain of mustard seed, the boy that thrust   10
His arm into the leaking dike to quell
The North Sea's onrush. Would you were not dust.⋄
With you I might invent, and make men try,
Some genuine shelter from this frantic sky.

published 1939

SECTION F
Richard Aldington

SECTION F: Poems by Richard Aldington

✦

Sunsets

The white body of the evening
Is torn into scarlet,
Slashed and gouged and seared
Into crimson,
And hung ironically   5
With garlands of mist.

And the wind
Blowing over London from Flanders
Has a bitter taste.

published 1915

Field Manoeuvres
Outpost duty

The long autumn grass under my body
Soaks my clothes with its dew;
Where my knees press into the ground
I can feel the damp earth.

In my nostrils is the smell of the crushed grass,   5
Wet pine-cones and bark.

Through the great bronze pine trunks
Glitters a silver segment of road.
Interminable squadrons of silver and blue horses
Pace in long ranks the blank fields of heaven.   10

There is no sound;
The wind hisses gently through the pine needles;
The flutter of a finch's wings about my head
Is like distant thunder,
And the shrill cry of a mosquito   15
Sounds loud and close.

I am 'to fire at the enemy column
After it has passed' –
But my obsolete rifle, loaded with 'blank',
Lies untouched before me,   20
My spirit follows after the gliding clouds,
And my lips murmur of the mother of beauty
Standing breast-high, in golden broom
Among the blue pine-woods!

                                        1916

Soliloquy – 1

No, I'm not afraid of death
(Not very much afraid, that is)
Either for others or myself;
Can watch them coming from the line
On the wheeled silent stretchers   5
And not shrink,
But munch my sandwich stoically
And make a joke, when 'it' has passed.

But – the way they wobble! –
God! that makes one sick.   10
Dead men should be so still, austere,
And beautiful,
Not wobbling carrion roped upon a cart …

Well, thank God for rum.

Soliloquy – 2

I was wrong, quite wrong;
The dead men are not always carrion.
After the advance,
As we went through the shattered trenches
Which the enemy had left,   5
We found, lying upon the fire-step,
A dead English soldier,
His head bloodily bandaged
And his closed left hand touching the earth,

More beautiful than one can tell,   10
More subtly coloured than a perfect Goya,°
And more austere and lovely in repose
Than Angelo's° hand could ever carve in stone.
                                                   1917

Picket

Dusk and deep silence …

Three soldiers huddled on a bench
Over a red-hot brazier,
And a fourth who stands apart
Watching the cold rainy dawn.   5

Then the familiar sound of birds –
Clear cock-crow, caw of rooks,
Frail pipe of linnet, the 'ting! ting!' of chaffinches,
And over all the lark
Outpiercing even the robin …   10

Wearily the sentry moves
Muttering the one word: 'Peace'.
                                        published 1919

Bombardment

Four days the earth was rent and torn
By bursting steel,
The houses fell about us;
Three nights we dared not sleep,
Sweating, and listening for the imminent crash   5
Which meant our death.

The fourth night every man,
Nerve-tortured, racked to exhaustion,
Slept, muttering and twitching,
While the shells crashed overhead.   10

The fifth day there came a hush;
We left our holes
And looked above the wreckage of the earth
To where the white clouds moved in silent lines
Across the untroubled blue.   15
                              published 1919

Living Sepulchres

One frosty night when the guns were still
I leaned against the trench
Making for myself *hokku*◊
Of the moon and flowers and of the snow.

But the ghostly scurrying of huge rats   5
Swollen with feeding upon men's flesh
Filled me with shrinking dread.
                              published 1919

Reserve

Though you desire me I will still feign sleep
And check my eyes from opening to the day,
For as I lie, thrilled by your gold-dark flesh,
I think of how the dead, my dead, once lay.

published 1919

Trench Idyll

We sat together in the trench,
He on a lump of frozen earth
Blown in the night before,
I on an unexploded shell;
And smoked and talked, like exiles,   5
Of how pleasant London was,
Its women, restaurants, night clubs, theatres,
How at that very hour
The taxi-cabs were taking folk to dine …
Then we sat silent for a while   10
As a machine-gun swept the parapet.

He said:
'I've been here on and off two years
And seen only one man killed.'

'That's odd.'   15

'The bullet hit him in the throat;
He fell in a heap on the fire-step,
And called out "My God! *dead*!"'

'Good Lord, how terrible!'

'Well, as to that, the nastiest job I've had   20

Was last year on this very front
Taking the discs° at night from men
Who'd hung for six months on the wire
Just over there.
The worst of all was   25
They fell to pieces at a touch.
Thank God we couldn't see their faces;
They had gas helmets on …'

I shivered;
'It's rather cold here, sir, suppose we move?'   30

published 1919

In the Trenches

1

Not that we are weary,
Not that we fear,
Not that we are lonely
Though never alone –
Not these, not these destroy us;   5
But that each rush and crash
Of mortar and shell,
Each cruel bitter shriek of bullet
That tears the wind like a blade,
Each wound on the breast of earth,   10
Of Demeter,° our Mother,
Wound us also,
Sever and rend the fine fabric
Of the wings of our frail souls,
Scatter into dust the bright wings   15
Of Psyche!°

2

Impotent,
How impotent is all this clamour,
This destruction and contest …
Night after night comes the moon   20

Haughty and perfect;
Night after night the Pleiades° sing
And Orion° swings his belt across the sky.
Night after night the frost
Crumbles the hard earth.   25

Soon the spring will drop flowers
And patient creeping stalk and leaf
Along these barren lines
Where the huge rats scuttle
And the hawk shrieks to the carrion crow.   30

Can you stay them with your noise?
Then kill winter with your cannon,
Hold back Orion with your bayonets
And crush the spring leaf with your armies!
                                    published 1919

Meditation

Outside the young frost crisps the grass
And bends the narrow willow boughs
And flecks the dyke with little spears of ice;
The huge moon, yellow and blotched,
Like the face of a six days' corpse,   5
Stares hideously over the barren wood.

In the silence, the deep pool-like silence,
Untroubled by crash of guns or tramp of men,
I sit alone in a small Belgian house
And stare against the moon and feel   10
Silence like a slow wave of the outer sea
Drive over and through me,
Purging out bitterness, effacing miseries.

I have what I yearned for –
The chance to live my life out to the end.   15
And it is a great joy to sit here quietly and think
That soon I shall return to her and say:

94

'Now it is a free man that kisses you'.
There will be strange meetings in cities for me,
The hush of summer in English gardens,   20
The glitter of spring in Italy,
The old cafés in Paris.

And I shall have books again,
Long quiet evenings by the tranquil lamp,
Or wild gaiety with 'my own sort' –   25
And always there will be her love,
Her eyes holding me dumb,
Her mouth drawing the blood to my lips.

And yet and yet
I am still not free from bitterness,   30
For as I sit here thinking so tenderly of her,
Maybe, over there across the Channel,
Her eyes smile at another man
As they smiled at me,
And her red mouth stabs him to passion   35
As it stabbed me.
Is any woman both beautiful and loyal?

I think also that I am too restless
For the old life,
Too contemptuous of narrow shoulders   40
To sit again with the café-chatterers,
Too sick at heart with overmuch slaughter
To dream quietly over books,
Too impatient of lies to cajole
Even my scanty pittance from the money-vultures.   45

Perhaps, then, this is my happiest moment,
Here in this cold little Belgian house,
Remembering harsh years past,
Plotting gold years to come,
Trusting so blithely in a woman's faith;   50
In the quiet night,
In the silence.

                                        1918

In the Palace Garden

The yews became a part of me,
The long walks edged with sparse flowers,
The fluttering green fringes of elm trees
Blurring the washed blue sky,
The long shivering ripples of the river,   5
Bird-calls, all we saw and did,
Became me, built me up,
Helped me to love you.
I was happy.
It was enough not to be dead,   10
Not to be a black spongy mass of decay
Half-buried on the edge of a trench,
More than enough to be young and gay,
To know my lips were such
Yours would be glad to meet them.   15
I loved you with my old miseries
Which were no longer miseries,
With the scent of the lilacs
And the softly sprinkling fountain,
And the kind glances of passers.   20
How did it happen then?
The sun did not cease shining,
The water rippled just as fleetly,
I loved you just as indiscreetly –
But gradually my golden mood tarnished,   25
Happiness hissed into nothing –
Metal under a fierce acid –
And I was whispering:
'This happiness is not yours;
It is stolen from other men.   30
Coward! You have shirked your fate'.

published 1923

Eumenides◦

It is at night one thinks,
At night, staring with sleepless eyes
At the narrow moonlit room.
Outside the owls hoot briefly,
And there are stars   5
Whose immortal order makes one shudder.

I do not need the ticking of my watch
To tell me I am mortal;
I have lived with, fed upon death
As happier generations feed on life;   10
My very mind seems gangrened.

What am I, lying here so still,
Staring till I almost see the silence?
What am I?
What obscure fragment of will?   15
What paltry life cell?

Have I not striven and striven for health?
Lived calmly (as it seemed) these many months,
Walked daily among neat hedged fields,
Watched the long pageant of the clouds,   20
Loved, drawn into my being, flowers,
English flowers – the thin anemones,
The honey drops of tufted primroses,
Wild scented hyacinths, white stitchwort,
The spotted orchis, tall scentless violets,   25
Larch buds, green and scarlet,
Noted the springing green
Of white ash, birch and heavy oak,
Lived with the noblest books, the noblest friends,
Looked gay, laughed free, worked long?   30

I have done all this,
And yet there are always nights
I lie awake staring with sleepless eyes,
And what is my mind's sickness,
What the agony I struggle with,   35
I can hardly tell.

Loos,° that horrible night in Hart's Crater,°
The damp cellars of Maroc,°
The frozen ghostly streets of Vermelles,°
That first night-long gas bombardment –   40
O the thousand images I see
And struggle with and cannot kill –
That boot I kicked
(It had a mouldy foot in it)
The night K's head was smashed   45
Like a rotten pear by a mortar,
The other night I trod on the dead man
And all the officers were hit ...

These, like Eumenides, glide about me,
Fearful memories of despair and misery,   50
Tortured flesh, caked blood, endurance,
Men, men and the roar of shells,
The hissing lights, red, green, yellow,
The clammy mud, the tortuous wire,
The slippery boards ...   55

It is all so stale,
It has been said a thousand times;
Millions have seen it, been it, as I;
Millions may be haunted by these spirits
As I am haunted;   60
May feel, as I feel, in the darkness,
Their flesh dripping into corruption,
Their youth and love and gaiety
Dissolved, violently slain, annihilated.

What is it I agonise for? 65
The dead? They are quiet;
They can have no complaint.
No, it is my own murdered self –
A self which had its passion for beauty,
Some moment's touch with immortality – 70
Violently slain, which rises up like a ghost
To torment my nights,
To pain me.
It is myself that is the Eumenides,
That will not be appeased, about my bed; 75
It is the wrong that has been done me
Which none has atoned for, none repented of,
Which rises before me, demanding atonement.

Tell me, what answer shall I give my murdered self?
                                  published 1923

Epilogue to 'Death of a Hero' *

Eleven years after the fall of Troy,
We, the old men – some of us nearly forty –
Met and talked on the sunny rampart
Over our wine, while the lizards scuttled
In dusty grass, and the crickets chirred. 5

Some bared their wounds;
Some spoke of the thirst, dry in the throat,
And the heart-beat, in the din of battle;
Some spoke of intolerable sufferings,
The brightness gone from their eyes 10
And the grey already thick in their hair.

And I sat a little apart
From the garrulous talk and old memories,
And I heard a boy of twenty
Say petulantly to a girl, seizing her arm: 15

'Oh, come away, why do you stand there
Listening open-mouthed to the talk of old men?
Haven't you heard enough of Troy and Achilles?°
Why should they bore us for ever
With an old quarrel and the names of dead men   20
We never knew, and dull forgotten battles?'

And he drew her away,
And she looked back and laughed
As he spoke more contempt of us,
Being now out of hearing.   25

And I thought of the graves by desolate Troy
And the beauty of many young men now dust,
And the long agony, and how useless it all was.
And the talk still clashed about me
Like the meeting of blade and blade.   30

And as they two moved further away
He put an arm about her, and kissed her;
And afterwards I heard their gay distant laughter.

And I looked at the hollow cheeks
And the weary eyes and the grey-streaked heads   35
Of the old men – nearly forty – about me;
And I too walked away
In an agony of helpless grief and pity.

published 1929

In Memory of Wilfred Owen

I had half-forgotten among the soft blue waters
And the gay-fruited arbutus° of the hill
Where never the nightingales are silent,
And the sunny hours are warm with honey and dew;

I had half-forgotten as the stars slid westward   5
Year after year in grave majestic order,
In the strivings and in the triumphs of manhood,
The world's voice, and the touch of beloved hands.

But I have never quite forgotten, never forgotten
All you who lie there so lonely, and never stir   10
When the hired buglers call unheeded to you,
Whom the sun shall never warm nor the frost chill.

Do you remember … but why should you remember?
Have you not given all you had, to forget?
Oh, blessed, blessed be Death! They can no more vex you,   15
You for whom memory and forgetfulness are one.

                                                    1931

SECTION G
Further Poems

◆

For the Guns

Pittendrigh MacGillivray

    'Good-bye, you fellows!' –
        And what more should be said?
In the thick of the shrapnel –
        In the hail of lead.
Intensely though gaily,   5
        Where the bullet-bees hum,
They step out – lots of thirty,
        As the word bids them come.

    'Good-bye, you fellows!' –
        And Life falls behind,   10
For in front there's a glitter
        Strikes Life from the mind.
And the guns draw their lovers,
        Clean-limbed every one,
Some cigarette-smoking,   15
        All game for the fun.

    'Good-bye, you fellows!' –
        For it's never again:
No more Piccadilly
        Nor the boom of Big Ben.   20

'Right here goes our innings –
   Not much of a show;
But the guns, boys, are waiting,
   So, quick, let us go: –
     Good-bye, you fellows!'   25
          1914

For the Fallen

Laurence Binyon

With proud thanksgiving, a mother for her children,
England mourns for her dead across the sea.
Flesh of her flesh they were, spirit of her spirit,
Fallen in the cause of the free.

Solemn the drums thrill: Death august and royal   5
Sings sorrow up into immortal spheres.
There is music in the midst of desolation
And a glory that shines upon our tears.

They went with songs to battle, they were young,
Straight of limb, true of eye, steady and aglow,   10
They were staunch to the end against odds uncounted,
They fell with their faces to the foe.

They shall grow not old, as we that are left grow old:
Age shall not weary them, nor the years condemn.
At the going down of the sun and in the morning   15
We will remember them.

They mingle not with their laughing comrades again;
They sit no more at familiar tables at home;
They have no lot in our labour of the day-time;
They sleep beyond England's foam.   20

But where our desires are and our hopes profound,
Felt as a well-spring that is hidden from sight,
To the innermost heart of their own land they are known
As the stars are known to the Night.

As the stars that shall be bright when we are dust,   25
Moving in marches upon the heavenly plain,
As the stars that are starry in the time of our darkness,
To the end, to the end, they remain.

                       1914

Spring in War-Time

Edith Nesbit

Now the sprinkled blackthorn snow
    Lies along the lovers' lane
Where last year we used to go –
    Where we shall not go again.

In the hedge the buds are new,   5
    By our wood the violets peer –
Just like last year's violets, too,
    But they have no scent this year.

Every bird has heart to sing
    Of its nest, warmed by its breast;   10
We had heart to sing last spring,
    But we never built our nest.

Presently red roses blown
    Will make all the garden gay …
Not yet have the daisies grown   15
    On your clay.

            1916

To His Love

Ivor Gurney

He's gone, and all our plans
   Are useless indeed.
We'll walk no more on Cotswold
   Where the sheep feed
   Quietly and take no heed.   5

His body that was so quick
   Is not as you
Knew it, on Severn river
   Under the blue
   Driving our small boat through.   10

You would not know him now ...
   But still he died
Nobly, so cover him over
   With violets of pride
   Purple from Severn side.   15

Cover him, cover him soon!
   And with thick-set
Masses of memoried flowers –
   Hide that red wet
   Thing I must somehow forget.   20
                published 1917

Easter Monday
(In Memoriam E.T.)◦

Eleanor Farjeon

In the last letter that I had from France
You thanked me for the silver Easter egg
Which I had hidden in the box of apples
You liked to munch beyond all other fruit.
You found the egg the Monday before Easter,   5
And said, 'I will praise Easter Monday now –
It was such a lovely morning.' Then you spoke
Of the coming battle and said, 'This is the eve.
Good-bye. And may I have a letter soon.'

That Easter Monday was a day for praise,   10
It was such a lovely morning. In our garden
We sowed our earliest seeds, and in the orchard
The apple-bud was ripe. It was the eve.
There are three letters that you will not get.

          1917

Picnic
July 1917

Rose Macaulay

We lay and ate sweet hurt-berries
    In the bracken of Hurt Wood.
Like a quire of singers singing low
    The dark pines stood.

Behind us climbed the Surrey hills,   5
    Wild, wild in greenery;
At our feet the downs of Sussex broke
    To an unseen sea.

And life was bound in a still ring,
    Drowsy, and quiet, and sweet …   10
When heavily up the south-east wind
    The great guns beat.

We did not wince, we did not weep,
    We did not curse or pray;
We drowsily heard, and someone said,   15
    'They sound clear today'.

We did not shake with pity and pain,
    Or sicken and blanch white.
We said, 'If the wind's from over there
    There'll be rain tonight'.   20

       . . . .

Once pity we knew, and rage we knew,
    And pain we knew, too well,
As we stared and peered dizzily
    Through the gates of hell.

But now hell's gates are an old tale;   25
    Remote the anguish seems;
The guns are muffled and far away,
    Dreams within dreams.

And far and far are Flanders mud,
    And the pain of Picardy;   30
And the blood that runs there runs beyond
    The wide waste sea.

We are shut about by guarding walls:
    (We have built them lest we run
Mad from dreaming of naked fear   35
    And of black things done).

We are ringed all round by guarding walls,
    So high, they shut the view.
Not all the guns that shatter the world
    Can quite break through.   40

      . . . .

Oh, guns of France, oh, guns of France,
    Be still, you crash in vain. …
Heavily up the south wind throb
    Dull dreams of pain, …

Be still, be still, south wind, lest your   45
    Blowing should bring the rain. …
We'll lie very quiet on Hurt Hill,
    And sleep once again.

Oh, we'll lie quite still, nor listen nor look,
    While the earth's bounds reel and shake,   50
Lest, battered too long, our walls and we
    Should break … should break. …
            published 1919

Field Ambulance in Retreat
Via Dolorosa, Via Sacra

May Sinclair

I

A straight flagged road, laid on the rough earth,
A causeway of stone from beautiful city to city,
Between the tall trees, the slender, delicate trees,
Through the flat green land, by plots of flowers, by black
     canals thick with heat.

II

The road-makers made it well   5
Of fine stone, strong for the feet of the oxen and of the great
     Flemish horses,
And for the high wagons piled with corn from the harvest.
And the labourers are few;
They and their quiet oxen stand aside and wait
By the long road loud with the passing of the guns, the rush
     of armoured cars, and the tramp of an army on the
     march forward to battle;   10
And, where the piled corn-wagons went, our dripping
     Ambulance carries home
Its red and white harvest from the fields.

III

The straight flagged road breaks into dust, into a thin white
     cloud,
About the feet of a regiment driven back league by league,   15
Rifles at trail, and standards wrapped in black funeral cloths.
Unhasting, proud in retreat,
They smile as the Red Cross Ambulance rushes by.
(You know nothing of beauty and of desolation who have
     not seen

That smile of an army in retreat.)   20
They go: and our shining, beckoning danger goes with them,
And our joy in the harvests that we gathered in at nightfall
        in the fields;
And like an unloved hand laid on a beating heart
Our safety weighs us down.
Safety hard and strange; stranger and yet more hard   25
As, league after dying league, the beautiful, desolate Land
Falls back from the intolerable speed of an Ambulance in retreat
On the sacred, dolorous Way.

                                                        1914

A Dead Boche

Robert Graves

To you who'd read my songs of War
    And only hear of blood and fame,
I'll say (you've heard it said before)
    'War's Hell!' and if you doubt the same,
To-day I found in Mametz Wood   5
A certain cure for lust of blood:

Where, propped against a shattered trunk,
    In a great mess of things unclean,
Sat a dead Boche; he scowled and stunk
    With clothes and face a sodden green,   10
Big-bellied, spectacled, crop-haired,
Dribbling black blood from nose and beard.

                                                        1916

Ypres

Herbert Read

1

With a chill and hazy light
   the sun of a winter noon
     swills
       thy ruins.

Thy ruins etched   5
   in silver silhouettes
     against a turquoise sky.

Lank poles leap to the infinite
   their broken wires
     tossed like the rat-locks of Maenades.   10

And Desolation broods over all
   gathering to her lap
     her leprous children.

The sparrows whimper
   amid the broken arches.   15

2

Sunset
   licks the ruins
     with vermeil flames.
The flames rise and fall
   against the dusking sky –   20
against the dusking sky
flames fall and die.

Heaped in the black night
   are the grey ashes
     of desolation.   25

But even now the moon
   blooms
     like a cankered rose
and with a soft passionate light
   kisses   30
     the wan harmonies of ruin.
           published 1926

Lament

W. W. Gibson

We who are left, how shall we look again
Happily on the sun, or feel the rain,
Without remembering how they who went
Ungrudgingly and spent
Their all for us, loved, too, the sun and rain?   5

A bird among the rain-wet lilac sings –
But we, how shall we turn to little things
And listen to the birds and winds and streams
Made holy by their dreams,
Nor feel the heart-break in the heart of things?   10
                  1919

from *Hugh Selwyn Mauberley*

Ezra Pound

These fought in any case,
and some believing,
    pro domo, in any case …

Some quick to arm,
some for adventure,   5
some from fear of weakness,
some from fear of censure,
some for love of slaughter, in imagination,
learning later …
some in fear, learning love of slaughter;   10

Died some, pro patria,
    non 'dulce' non 'et decor' …
walked eye-deep in hell
believing in old men's lies, then unbelieving
came home, home to a lie,   15
home to many deceits,
home to old lies and new infamy;
usury age-old and age-thick
and liars in public places.

Daring as never before, wastage as never before.   20
Young blood and high blood,
fair cheeks, and fine bodies;

fortitude as never before

frankness as never before,
disillusions as never told in the old days,   25
hysterias, trench confessions,
laughter out of dead bellies.

There died a myriad,
And of the best, among them,
For an old bitch gone in the teeth,   30
For a botched civilization,

Charm, smiling at the good mouth,
Quick eyes gone under earth's lid,

For two gross of broken statues,
For a few thousand battered books.   35
                              1919

GLOSSARY AND NOTES ON THE POEMS

Edward Thomas

The Owl (p. 13)

14   **sobered:** given food for thought.

A Private (p. 13)

title   an ordinary infantry soldier.

4–6   **Hawthorn Bush … The Drover:** typical names of country inns.

6   **a hundred spot the down:** 'a hundred bushes can be seen growing like spots on the surface of the downland.'

This is No Case of Petty Right or Wrong (p. 14)

5   **one fat patriot:** a reference to the poet's father.

6   **Kaiser:** Wilhelm II, Kaiser (King) of Germany until his abdication at the end of the Great War.

19   **ken:** knowledge or understanding.

The Sun Used to Shine (p. 15)

1   **we two:** a reference to Edward Thomas himself and the American poet Robert Frost, a close friend who persuaded Thomas to turn to writing poetry.

17   **Hades:** the underworld.

21   **the Crusades:** military campaigns during the eleventh to thirteenth centuries to try to recapture the Holy Land for Christianity from Islam.

22   **Caesar's battles:** Julius Caesar, whose military campaigns across Europe helped to establish the Roman Empire.

Roads (p. 17)

33   **Helen:** the name of the poet's wife; also a reference to a Roman road in Wales called 'Sarn Helen'.

35   **Mabinogion:** a collection of medieval Welsh myths and legends.

48   **chanticleer:** a name given in fairy tales, etc. to a farmyard cockerel.

'Home' (p. 19)

7   **league:** a long distance; about three miles.

As the Team's Head Brass (p. 21)

1   **head brass:** the brass buckles, bits and ornaments on the harness of the horses pulling the plough.

6   **charlock:** wild mustard

10   **share:** the ploughshare; the cutting blade of the plough.

Isaac Rosenberg

In Piccadilly (p. 26)

title   in Rosenberg's day, one of the smartest and busiest streets in London.

The Dead Heroes (p. 26)

6   **seraphim:** angelic beings, often presented as figures in armour.

Marching (p. 29)

sub title   **file:** a row of men marching in a column made up of several files.

10   **Mars:** in Greek mythology, the God of War.

Break of Day in the Trenches (p. 30)

2   **druid:** an ancient Celtic priest; here, associated with the remote past.

8   **cosmopolitan:** not limited to one country or nationality.

Louse Hunting (p. 31)

20 **Highland fling:** a very lively Scottish dance.

Dead Man's Dump (p. 33)

1 **limbers:** the detachable front part of a gun-carriage.

32 **pyre:** a bonfire for cremating corpses.

34 **ichor:** in Greek mythology, a fluid flowing like blood through the veins of the gods.

Wilfred Owen

1914 (p. 38)

3 **Berlin:** the capital of Prussia and of Imperial Germany, where the court and government of Kaiser Wilhelm II was located.

9–10 **Greece … Rome:** Owen is referring to the development of European civilisation.

Nocturne (p. 38)

title a picture of a night scene; a short piece of romantic piano music.

Anthem for Doomed Youth (p. 39)

1 **passing-bells:** the bell that tolls to announce a death.

4 **orisons:** prayers.

8 **sad shires:** many of the regiments to which soldiers with the British Expeditionary Force belonged were named after counties (shires).

Dulce et Decorum Est (p. 40)

title 'It is sweet and honourable [to die for one's country]'; from an ode by the Roman poet Horace.

8 **Five-Nines:** explosive shells.

25 **My friend:** Owen entitled an earlier draft of this poem 'To Jessie Pope etc.' Jessie Pope was a writer of popular patriotic verse during the First World War.

The Next War (p. 41)

10   **leagued:** teamed up with; collaborated.

The Chances (p. 42)

10   **Fritz:** a British army slang name for the German enemy.

12   **blighty:** a wound serious enough to put a soldier out of the war but not to kill him; 'Blighty' meant 'Britain' or 'home'.

The Sentry (p. 42)

1   **Boche:** originally a French slang-word meaning 'rascal'; during the Great War applied to German soldiers or to the German army generally (see Robert Graves, 'A Dead Boche', p. 111).

Exposure (p. 44)

3   **salient:** a point in a line of military attack or defence where the line bulges outwards towards the enemy.

26   **glozed:** here meaning 'glazed' and 'glowed'; normally meaning 'making something sound better than it is'.

S.I.W. (p. 45)

title   'Self Inflicted Wound'.

10   **Y. M. Hut:** Y.M.C.A.; the Young Men's Christian Association, an organisation which during the war ran rest huts providing recreation and counselling facilities for soldiers.

17   **trench-foot:** a serious skin complaint, partly caused by soldiers' having to wear waterlogged boots in the Trenches for long periods.

18   **untrapped:** provided an excuse for the soldier to leave the Trenches.

28   **the English ball:** a bullet manufactured in England.

30   **thrall:** enslavement.

31   **infrangibly:** 'unbreakably'.

The Send-Off (p. 47)

8   **the upland camp:** a training camp in England, possibly at Ripon, where Wilfred Owen was stationed before returning to France in 1918.

16   **great bells:** the celebrations at the end of the war.

Futility (p. 48)

9   **a cold star:** the earth, woken into life by the sun.

Strange Meeting (p. 48)

3   **titanic:** on a huge scale; from 'Titans', the earliest race of gods according to Greek mythology.

13   **flues:** chimneys; cracks leading to the air above.

Smile, Smile, Smile (p. 50)

title the refrain of a popular First World War song, 'Pack up your troubles in your old kit bag and smile, smile, smile'.

2   *Mail: The Daily Mail*, one of the most widely read news-papers during the Great War.

3   **Vast Booty from our Latest Haul:** the exaggeration of good news from the Front to keep up morale at home.

22   **England:** those who really represented what was best in their country, i.e. the ordinary soldiers fighting in the Trenches.

Spring Offensive (p. 51)

20   **begird:** prepare for battle physically and mentally.

39   **drave:** 'drove'.

Siegfried Sassoon

The Hero (p. 56)

15   **Wicked Corner:** many trenches and locations on the Front Line were given unofficial names by the troops.

The General (p. 58)

6   **Arras:** the Battle of Arras, April 1917.

Base Details (p. 58)

6   **Roll of Honour:** the list of casualties published in the news-
     papers. After the Great War, the Roll of Honour was the list
     of dead from each town, village, school, etc., usually re-
     corded on a war memorial.

Song-Books of the War (p. 59)

17   **Haig's last drive:** Earl Haig was commander of the British Ex-
     peditionary Force in France from 1915 to 1918. He was re-
     sponsible for maintaining the policy of war by attrition along
     the Western Front. He was in charge of the final offensive
     which drove the Germans back behind the Hindenberg Line
     and led to the end of fighting.

Counter-Attack (p. 61)

5   **Lewis guns:** light machine-guns.

16   **the Allemands:** the Germans.

26   **fire-step:** the raised position from which soldiers could fire
     over the top of a trench.

Glory of Women (p. 62)

5   **You make us shells:** women worked in the munitions fac-
     tories during the war.

8   **laurelled:** crowned with the laurels of victory; here used ironi-
     cally to imply that to the women all the dead soldiers are he-
     roes.

Aftermath (p. 63)

10   **Mametz:** scene of fierce fighting during the Battle of the
     Somme, 1916.

To One Who Was With Me in the War (p. 65)

9   **redoubt:** in military terms, a fortification in front of the main line of defences.

32   **enfilades:** directs machine gun fire along a line from end to end.

On Passing the New Menin Gate (p. 67)

1   **Gate:** at Ypres a ceremonial gateway which forms the Allied memorial and which is inscribed with the names of thousands of the known dead from the war.

Edmund Blunden

Festubert: the Old German Line (p. 70)

title   Festubert is a village near Béthune. Blunden was stationed here on arrival in France. It was the scene of fierce fighting in 1915 and again in 1918.

6   **malison:** a curse.

The Unchangeable (p. 70)

2   **Ancre:** a river which joins the Somme; scene of a fierce battle in November 1915.

3   **becks:** streams

Les Halles d'Ypres (p. 71)

title   The Halls of Ypres. Ypres, once a major Belgian town, rich and famous for its weaving industry, centred on the Cloth Hall. Ypres was the scene of fierce fighting and destruction throughout the Great War.

5   **Saint Martin's spire:** the spire of the cathedral which was destroyed by shelling.

7   **the Cloth Hall:** 'One of the finest Gothic public buildings in Belgium ... but now a scarcely recognizable ruin' (Muirhead, *Blue Guide to Belgium and the Western Front*, 1920).

The Sentry's Mistake (p. 74)

15   His up-and-down sans cursed bundook and spike: the sentry
paces up and down on his beat without carrying his hated
rifle and bayonet.

The Zonnebeke Road (p. 75)

title   a road leading to the village of Zonnebeke, between Ypres
and Passchendaele.

16   saturnine: dark and forbidding.

17   Haymarket: a street in London; the name given by British soldiers to a communication trench near the Zonnebeke Road.

19   minenwerfers: small black trench mortars which hovered me-
nacingly in the air before coming down.

26   gargoyle: a carved grotesque figure on the outside of a church
building, usually with an open mouth through which water
from the gutters can drain out.

28   bine: the twisting stem of a climbing plant.

Concert Party: Busseboom (p. 76)

title   concert parties (groups of actors and musicians) were a popular form of entertainment for troops resting behind the lines
during the Great War.

17   Saint Eloi: a village south of Ypres.

23   in the tunnels below Larch Wood: both sides used to dig tunnels out into No Man's Land to try to mine the enemy's trenches. Larch Wood is now the site of an allied war cemetery.

Vlamertinghe: Passing the Chateau, July 1917 (p. 77)

title   a large village on the way to Ypres. It was almost totally destroyed by four years of artillery fire.

Illusions (p. 78)

13   malkins: scarecrows.

Third Ypres (p. 80)

5   **fascined:** a fascine is a long faggot (bundle of sticks) used in war for lining trenches, ditches, etc.

33   **unplashed hedge:** a hedge that has not been properly laid or trimmed but allowed to grow wild.

71   **pollard:** a tree whose branches and twigs have been cut right back to the stem.

98   **lyddite:** high explosive used in shells. The name comes from the town of Lydd in Kent.

Premature Rejoicing (p. 84)

2   **Thiepval Wood:** scene of fierce fighting during the summer of 1916.

5   **Titania:** the Fairy Queen in Shakespeare's *A Midsummer Night's Dream*.

To W.O. and his Kind (p. 86)

title   W.O. is Wilfred Owen. Blunden did not meet Owen, but edited his *Collected Poems* in 1931.

12   **Would you were not dust:** 'I wish you were not dead.'

Richard Aldington

Soliloquy – 2 (p. 90)

11   **Goya:** a Spanish artist (1746–1828).

13   **Angelo:** Michelangelo (1475–1564), the pre-eminent Italian sculptor and painter.

Living Sepulchres (p. 91)

3   **hokku:** haiku, a Japanese verse form consisting of seventeen syllables.

Trench Idyll (p. 92)

22   **discs:** identification tags.

In the Trenches (p. 93)

11   **Demeter:** in Greek mythology, the Corn Goddess.

16   **Psyche:** in Greek mythology, a nymph beloved by Cupid; the Soul, sometimes represented as a butterfly.

22   **Pleiades:** a cluster of stars known as 'The Seven Sisters'.

23   **Orion:** the Hunter – a constellation.

Eumenides (p. 97)

title   in Greek tragedy, the Eumenides are the Furies who, in the *Oresteia* of Aeschylus, pursue Orestes for killing his mother after she had murdered his father Agamemnon. They were represented in Greek mythology as merciless goddesses of vengeance.

37–9   **Loos ... Hart's Crater ... Maroc ... Vermelles:** the Battle of Loos took place in September and October 1915, and there was further fighting in this area and around the villages of Maroc and Vermelles in 1917 and 1918. Hart's Crater was one of the most notorious battlefield mine craters in northern France.

Epilogue to 'Death of a Hero' (p. 99)

title   *Death of a Hero*: Richard Aldington's novel about the First World War, published in 1929.

18   **Achilles:** the Greek hero, killed during the siege of Troy.

In Memory of Wilfred Owen (p. 101)

2   **gay-fruited arbutus:** an evergreen tree with strawberry-like berries.

Further Poems

For the Guns (p. 103)

Author: Pittendrigh MacGillivray. Scots poet and historian; this poem was published in a collection entitled *Pro Patria* (1915).

For the Fallen (p. 104)

Author: Laurence Binyon (1869–1943), poet and Orientalist. This poem was written in the second month of the war. Its fourth stanza is still recited at Remembrance Day services.

Spring in War-Time (p. 105)

Author: Edith Nesbit (1858–1924). Poet and children's novelist.

To His Love (p. 106)

Author: Ivor Gurney (1890–1937). Composer and poet.

Easter Monday (p. 107)

Author: Eleanor Farjeon (1881–1965). Children's writer; a close friend of Edward Thomas, to whom this poem is dedicated, and of his wife Helen.

Picnic (p. 108)

Author: Rose Macaulay (1889–1958). Novelist, essayist and poet.

Field Ambulance in Retreat (p. 110)

Author: May Sinclair (1865–1946). Novelist; during the Great War she served with the Red Cross in a Field Ambulance Corps in Belgium.

A Dead Boche (p. 111)

Author: Robert Graves (1895–1993). Poet, novelist and critic; a close friend and fellow soldier of Siegfried Sassoon; the author of *Goodbye to All That* (1929).

Ypres (p. 112)

Author: Herbert Read (1893–1968). Poet, writer, art critic; a lifelong friend of Richard Aldington.

Lament (p. 113)

Author: W. W. Gibson (1878–1960). Poet; an early member of the Georgian poets; close friend of Edward Thomas and Rupert Brooke.

from **Hugh Selwyn Mauberley (p. 114)**

Author: Ezra Pound (1885–1972). American poet and critic; between 1912 and 1920 he led the English literary avant-garde, launching Richard Aldington's career and helping to establish Imagism as a poetry movement.

THE GREAT WAR: events in Europe	EDWARD THOMAS (1878–1917)	WILFRED OWEN (1893–1918)	ISAAC ROSENBERG (1890–1918)	EDMUND BLUNDEN (1896–1974)	SIEGFRIED SASSOON (1886–1967)	RICHARD ALDINGTON (1892–1962)
			May: leaves Slade Art School. Sails to S. Africa.			August: tries to enlist, but turned down on medical grounds. Working as writer and reviewer in London.
4 August: Britain declares war against Germany.	August: working as freelance writer.	August: in France working as a private tutor.			3 August: enlists as a trooper in the Sussex Yeomanry, the day before the outbreak of war.	
23 August: British Expeditionary Force (BEF) in retreat from Mons.						
September: Battle of the Marne.				September: pupil at Christ's Hospital, Sussex.		
October-November: First Battle of Ypres.						
	December: sends drafts of first poems to Robert Frost.					

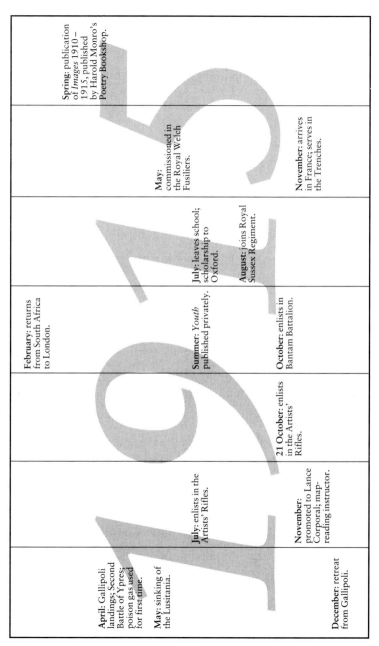

Spring: publication of *Images* 1910–1915, published by Harold Monro's Poetry Bookshop.

May: commissioned in the Royal Welch Fusiliers.

November: arrives in France; serves in the Trenches.

July: leaves school; scholarship to Oxford.

August: joins Royal Sussex Regiment.

February: returns from South Africa to London.

Summer: *Youth* published privately.

October: enlists in Bantam Battalion.

21 October: enlists in the Artists' Rifles.

July: enlists in the Artists' Rifles.

November: promoted to Lance Corporal; map-reading instructor.

April: Gallipoli landings; Second Battle of Ypres; poison gas used for first time.

May: sinking of the Lusitania.

December: retreat from Gallipoli.

THE GREAT WAR: events in Europe	EDWARD THOMAS (1878–1917)	WILFRED OWEN (1893–1918)	ISAAC ROSENBERG (1890–1918)	EDMUND BLUNDEN (1896–1974)	SIEGFRIED SASSOON (1886–1967)	RICHARD ALDINGTON (1892–1962)
January: conscription introduced.	March: promoted to Corporal.	February – March: in lodgings over Harold Monro's Poetry Bookshop, London.	March: transfers to 11th King's Own Royal Lancasters.	May: receives Commission; goes to France; in the Trenches at Festubert.		June: conscripted; joins 11th Devonshire Regiment in Dorset.
May: naval Battle of Jutland.		4 March: shows poems to Monro.				
July: Battle of the Somme begins.		4 June: commissioned into the Manchester Regiment.	3 June: arrives in France; first experience of the Trenches.	June: publication of *Pastorals*.	June: awarded the Military Cross; sick leave in England.	
			Summer: writes 'August 1914'.	August: battalion moves to the Somme.	August: begins writing satirical poems against the war.	
September: tanks used for first time.	September: Officer Cadet with the Royal Artillery. November: commissioned 2nd Lieutenant. December: volunteers for overseas service. Sends set of poems, later published under pseudonym of Edward Eastaway, to Robert Frost.	September: applies unsuccessfully for transfer to Royal Flying Corps. 29 December: crosses to France with 5th Manchesters.	December: 'Marching' and 'Break of Day in the Trenches' published in *Poetry* (Chicago).	13 November: awarded the Military Cross.		December: sent to France as a non-commissioned officer.

29 January: embarkation for France.	1 January: arrives at the Somme; joins 2nd Manchesters near Beaumont Hamel.	February: reassigned to Royal Engineers, working with wiring parties by night in No Man's Land.		February: returns to France.	March: applies for commission; continues at the Front until April; returns to England on leave.
11 February: takes up position near Arras.	March: evacuated from the Front to military hospital with concussion.				
9 March: begins duty at Observation Post (Ronville).	April: rejoins battalion.			April: wounded in shoulder, invalided back to England.	
9 April: killed by shell during first hour of the Arras offensive.	2 May: evacuated to Casualty Clearing Station with shell shock.				
April: Battle of Arras; capture of Vimy Ridge.	26 June: arrives Craiglockhart War Hospital, near Edinburgh.			June: publishes public protest against the war.	June: begins officer training.
April: United States of America declares war on Germany.	August: meets Siegfried Sassoon at Craiglockhart.		July – October: takes part in third Ypres offensive; gassed twice.	July: sent to Craiglockhart Hospital, Edinburgh.	
July: Third Battle of Ypres, Passchendaele.	13 October: introduced by Sassoon to Robert Graves.	September: last home leave in London.		August: first meeting with Wilfred Owen.	August: *Reverie*, poems written in the Trenches, published.
November: Battle of Cambrai.	24 November: rejoins 5th Manchesters at Scarborough for light duties.	November: in action during Battle of Cambrai; in hospital with influenza.		November: passed fit again for active service.	December: commissioned with 3rd Royal Sussex Regiment.
November: Russian Revolution.					

THE GREAT WAR: events in Europe	EDWARD THOMAS (1878–1917)	WILFRED OWEN (1893–1918)	ISAAC ROSENBERG (1890–1918)	EDMUND BLUNDEN (1896–1974)	SIEGFRIED SASSOON (1886–1967)	RICHARD ALDINGTON (1892–1962)
March: German offensive in Picardy. **May:** German offensive on the Aisne. **15 July:** German Champagne–Marne offensive. **18 July:** Allied counter-offensive on the Marne. **8 August:** Battle of Amiens begins. **15 August:** British troops cross the Ancre. **30 August:** British troops cross the Somme. **28 September:** Allied advance in Flanders begins. **29 September:** British and Empire forces begin attack on Hindenberg Line. **9 November:** Kaiser Wilhelm II of Germany abdicates. **11 November:** Armistice between the allies and Germany.		**26 January:** first poem, 'The Miners', to be published in *The Nation*. **March:** stationed in Ripon. **5 June:** rejoins 5th Manchesters at Scarborough. **15 June:** 'Hospital Barge' and 'Futility', published in *The Nation*. **August:** embarkation leave; visits Sassoon in hospital. **31 August:** returns to France. **September:** at Amiens. **29 September:** in action at Beaurevoir-Fonsomme; awarded Military Cross. **4 November:** killed in action during attack across Oise-Sambre Canal. **11 November:** news of Owen's death reaches parents in Shrewsbury.	**January:** returns to the Trenches. **1 April:** killed at the Front.	**Spring:** posted to a training centre in Suffolk. **June:** marries, aged 21.	**February:** posted to Palestine. **May:** rejoins Battalion in France. **July:** receives head wound; invalided out of France.	**Spring:** returns to France; shell-shocked and gassed in the Trenches. **September:** returns to the Front; Battalion Signals Officer in Belgium at time of the Armistice.

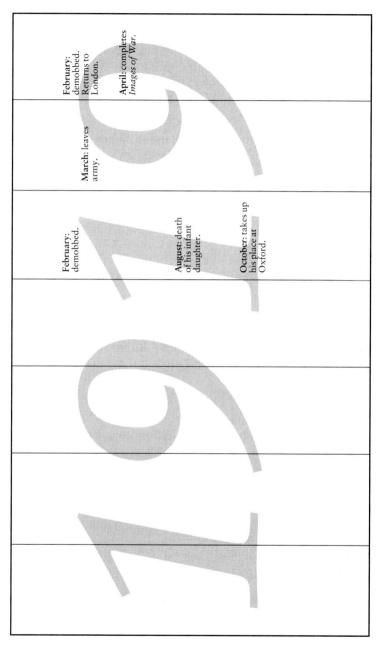

February: demobbed. Returns to London.

April: completes *Images of War*.

March: leaves army.

February: demobbed.

August: death of his infant daughter.

October: takes up his place at Oxford.

RESOURCE NOTES

Who has written these poems and why?

It is easy to assume that the soldier poets of the Great War were somehow all alike: ex-public school boys, privileged products of Edwardian England, officers and gentlemen. In fact, these six poets came from varied backgrounds and had different motives for fighting. Four of them originally served as private soldiers, though five were eventually to become commissioned officers. What they had in common was that they all experienced the extreme conditions of life on the Western Front, and they all went to France determined that the war should not prevent them from developing as poets.

Only Siegfried Sassoon came from a really privileged background. He was educated at Marlborough public school and Cambridge University, and then lived the life of a country gentleman until 1914. Edmund Blunden, who had also been educated at a public school (Christ's Hospital), was the son of a schoolmaster. Although he had won a classics scholarship to Oxford University, he decided to join the army. Edward Thomas went to Oxford University, but had already married and become a father by the time he took his degree. Richard Aldington went to London University, but had to leave after his father went bankrupt. Wilfred Owen, whose father had a poorly paid job on the railways, failed to win the scholarship he needed to study at Reading University. Isaac Rosenberg, who was brought up in poverty in the Jewish East End of London, left school at 15 to be apprenticed to an engraver. Eventually, after attending evening classes, he won a place at the Slade School of Art.

Owen had been in France when war was declared. Rosenberg was in South Africa. Neither was inclined to join up at first, unlike Sassoon, who had enlisted the day before war broke out, and Blunden, who joined as an officer cadet as soon as he left school. Thomas was old enough not to have enlisted at all; his decision had as much to do with the need to escape personal and financial pressures as with a desire to fight for his country, although that too was important. 'Literally for this,' he replied, holding up a clod of English soil, when a friend asked what he was fighting for. Aldington had tried to enlist at the start of the war, but was turned down on medical grounds; in 1916 he was conscripted anyway. Rosenberg finally joined up because he could make no money from his painting or writing.

By the time they joined the army, all six thought of themselves as serious writers. Thomas had turned to writing poetry at the suggestion of a friend, the American poet Robert Frost, but he did not live to see any of his poems published. Blunden, Sassoon and Rosenberg had all published poems in small privately-printed editions. Owen had published nothing as yet. Aldington had published his first volume, *Images*, in 1915, and already had a growing reputation as a member of the literary avant-garde in London.

Apart from Aldington, these writers were (or have later been) associated with the Georgian poets: young writers whose work was admired and promoted by Edward Marsh, Winston Churchill's secretary and editor of the *Georgian Poetry* anthologies which appeared between 1912 and 1922. None of them, however, had been published by Marsh before joining the army. Owen thought his career as a poet was established once he could say, 'I am held peer by the Georgians,' although his work never actually appeared in *Georgian Poetry*. Edward Thomas was another who never appeared in the anthologies, but whose work shared the hallmarks of Georgian poetry at its best: a focus on the English countryside and on the lives of ordinary people; clear, up-to-date diction; and emphasis on shorter lyrics rather than long poems.

After the war, those who had been killed had their poems published in collected editions, often edited by the other

Georgians. It took many years, however, for the importance of Thomas and Rosenberg to be properly recognised. Aldington and Sassoon had volumes of war poetry published almost at once; Blunden in 1922. All three wrote important novels or memoirs of the war which appeared a decade or so later. Aldington lived entirely by his writing for the rest of his life; Blunden by writing and teaching; Sassoon partly by writing and partly from private means. For each of them, the war remained, in a sense, the great event of their lives, one which they constantly re-visited and, to an extent, exorcised through poetry.

✦ Activities and discussion

1 Study the Date Chart (pp. 128–133). How far did the six poets share the same experiences of the Great War? How far do their poems – their titles and their themes – seem to you to reflect their experiences as soldiers?

2 There are many questions that can be asked about each war poem. Read 'For the Guns' (p. 103). This poem was written in 1914 and published in a book called *Pro Patria* ('For the sake of one's country'). Now answer the following questions about the poem:

a Is the writer presenting his poem from the viewpoint of a soldier or a civilian?

b At what sort of reader or listener is the poem aimed?

c What response do you think the writer is hoping the poem will provoke?

d How do you react to the poem?

e How do you think the poem would have been received in 1914? In 1918?

f Do you enjoy/admire some parts of the poem but not others?

g Are there features of the poem which you find disturbing/ revealing/amusing?

3 Now read three other poems written near the start of the war (or relating to that time), for example '1914' by Owen (p. 38), 'This is No Case of Petty Right or Wrong' by Thomas (p. 14) or 'A Letter Home' by Sassoon (p. 54). Try answering the same questions about these poems as you answered about 'For the Guns'. Compare your answers. Which of the questions make you think most carefully about each poem?

4 Many of the poems in this collection use the first person ('I'). Usually the 'I' will seem to refer to the poet. Can you be sure that this is so? Are there poems in which the poet seems to be speaking as somebody else?

5 Imagine that a newspaper in 1917 decided to write a feature about war poets, and wanted to interview each of the six poets in this book while they were home on leave. Working in a group, think of questions you might ask to get each poet to:
   • talk frankly about his experiences at the Front;
   • explain and justify the way he has written about the war in his poems.

One member of the group should then take the part of each poet and try to answer the questions put by the other members of the group ('hotseating'). The answers given to each question should, as far as possible, reflect what the poets wrote in the poems you have read.

◆

What type of texts are these poems?

The poems in this edition were all written by poets who happened also to become soldiers for the duration of the Great War, or until they were killed. The poems are about war: about the fear of fighting; about the fighting itself; about the conditions that soldiers endured before, during or after battle. They are about the effects that war had on them and on other people, and about the impact that war continued to have long after it was over on those who had experienced it.

Some of the poems were written before the poet went to war, some in the Trenches or while on leave from the fighting. Others, a surprising number, were written after the war was over.

Before the twentieth century, most poems written about war celebrated patriotism, self-sacrifice and heroism – whether in victory or defeat. For readers at the end of the nineteenth century, war poetry was hardly a special category of writing, as it is today. There was not a single poet from Shakespeare to Tennyson whose reputation rested largely or solely on the poems written about war. Rarely were the poets who wrote about war also soldiers; even if they were, they did not report on their experience as soldiers in the way that, for example, Rosenberg or Owen did. War poetry, as the term is understood today, was really born in the Great War.

These poems focus on several key themes: the effect of war on nature and on the landscape, especially the landscape of the Western Front – the Trenches, No Man's Land, the ruined towns and villages; the way individuals coped with the violence of battle and the presence of death; the gulf between people at home – families, politicians and those who peddled propaganda – and the men and women at the Front; the guilt of surviving when others around them were dying. Each poem, whether it is recording actual events and incidents or whether it is reflecting on some aspect of the war, is an attempt to make sense of a world where 'normal life' has been replaced by something that can only be fully understood by those who have experienced it at first hand.

These poems are therefore evidence. Along with contemporary photographs, paintings, newspaper reports, letters and diaries, they give a picture of what, for certain people, the Great War was actually like. They explain how these people felt about the war and how they reacted to it. Some poets, for example Owen, consciously wrote for future generations. Historians can make use of the poems as source material, and may ask of these texts, 'Are they reliable as evidence? In what sense do they give a *true* picture of the Great War? Do they speak for all soldiers, or only for those soldiers who were also poets and felt about the war in a certain way?'

It is also worth asking, 'When were these poems written? Does it matter that some poets, for example Blunden, used their diaries and their recollections to re-create events and thoughts that had first occurred five or ten years previously? How important is memory in all these poems?' The three poets in this edition who survived the war – Sassoon, Blunden and Aldington – all went on to write memoirs or novels about the Great War: *Memoirs of an Infantry Officer*, *Undertones of War* and *Death of a Hero*. Each had a great impact on the way later generations imagined the war to have been. It took ten years for these books to appear. During that decade, however, each of the writers continued to write poetry about the war and about their memory of it. The war haunted them, and at first they were able to exorcise it only through writing poems, not prose.

Wilfred Owen famously said, 'Above all I am not concerned with Poetry.' However, to read these texts today simply as historical evidence is to ignore what makes them different from other artefacts of the Great War. They are poems, written by people who thought of themselves as poets, and who used language in a particular way. In every poem meaning, diction (the poet's choice and use of words), imagery and form interact with one another, and all these elements are part of the whole. In the end, it is important to decide whether these are simply poems which happen to be about war or whether they have some unique ingredient which makes them 'war poetry'.

✦ Activities and discussion

1 Choose five poems, either by one poet or by different poets, each of which looks at a different aspect of the war. What do these poems have in common? If you had come across any one of these poems unexpectedly, would you have known it was a 'war poem'?

2 In what ways do the poems composed before their writers went to France differ from those written later on, either during or after the war? Look, for example, at Owen's '1914' (p. 38) and 'The Send-Off' (p. 47), or Aldington's 'Sunsets' (p. 88) and 'Bombardment' (p. 91).

3 What are the ingredients you look for in war poetry? Explore the poems in Section G: Further Poems. What are the main differences, if any, between the poems written by poets who also fought (i.e. Herbert Read, Ivor Gurney, Robert Graves), and those who remained civilians?

4 In 1981, *Scars Upon My Heart*, an anthology of poems by women during the Great War, was published. In the preface one of the editors asked the question:

> Is there among men, not excluding editors of war-poetry anthologies, the atavistic feeling that war is man's concern, as birth is woman's; and that women simply cannot speak on the matter?

Read the poems by women writers in Section G, then try through a formal debate or informal discussion to come to a conclusion about whether war poems can also be written by women.

5 Edward Thomas's poems were all written before he saw action in the Trenches. How much, if anything, do his poems have in common with the poems of Rosenberg or Blunden? Compare 'Home' (p. 19) with 'Returning, We Hear the Larks' (p. 32) and with 'The Sentry's Mistake' (p. 74).

6 Many of the poems in this book describe a single event or scene from the war. Sometimes the poet would write the poem well after the event, referring to letters or a diary to recall exact details. Choose one of the following poems, and read it carefully. Then rewrite the events described in it as if in a diary entry or in a letter:
   • Edward Thomas, 'The Owl' (p. 13);
   • Isaac Rosenberg, 'Louse Hunting' (p. 31);
   • Wilfred Owen, 'Exposure' (p. 44);
   • Siegfried Sassoon, 'A Working Party' (p. 57);
   • Edmund Blunden, 'Les Halles d'Ypres' (p. 71);
   • Richard Aldington, 'Meditation' (p. 94).

✦

How were these poems produced?

> I am going up to the trenches very shortly ... and I mean to
> suck in all I can when I get up there. I am always trying to im-
> press things on my memory, and make as many notes as I can.
> (Siegfried Sassoon, in a letter to Edward Marsh,
> March 1916)

War poems are rarely written in the heat of battle; like most
poems they are composed after the events they describe. In the
Great War, the poets wrote in the few moments of relative
peace they could snatch. Edmund Blunden, like many soldiers,
kept a diary. He used this in the years after the war to write
his poems and his memoir *Undertones of War*. Isaac Rosenberg
managed to write and revise poems while he was out in France,
but had great difficulty posting them back to England: the
censors who checked all the letters sent by private soldiers told
him they did not have time to read 'rubbish'. Nevertheless, he
persevered:

> I am determined that this war, with all its powers for devasta-
> tion, shall not master my poeting; that is, if I am lucky enough
> to come through all right. I will not leave a corner of my con-
> sciousness covered up, but saturate myself with the strange and
> extraordinary new conditions of this life, and it will all refine it-
> self into poetry later on.
> (Isaac Rosenberg, in a letter to Laurence Binyon, 1917)

Letters were a vital means of recording experience close to the
events, and Wilfred Owen wrote many letters, to his mother
and to his cousin, which contained material that he later
transformed into poetry, particularly while he was on sick
leave back in England. It seems that being out of the Trenches,
and especially being back in England, helped the poets to focus
more clearly on what they had endured in France.

At the same time, their dismay, which later became anger,
at the way people at home failed to appreciate the reality of

fighting on the Western Front, made the task of explaining all the more urgent. Often the poems which seem most strongly 'anti-war' are really attacking those who defended or glorified the war, rather than the concept of war itself. Wilfred Owen's poem 'Dulce et Decorum Est' was first drafted in Scotland, where Owen was recovering from shell-shock at Craiglockhart Hospital, and completed later in Yorkshire. Originally it was to have been dedicated, ironically, to Jessie Pope, a writer whose jingoistic war poems were immensely popular, especially with children.

All the writers spent several months in training camps in England before going to France; sometimes they were sent behind the lines or back to England for further training after months in the Trenches. Edward Thomas found more time to write poetry in camp than he had done as a civilian. Some of Richard Aldington's poems describe his experiences and feelings while undergoing training.

Getting their poems published while in France was a problem for all the poets. Owen had a few published in magazines and journals, but was more concerned with building up a collection of poems that would be published, after the war or after his death, in a single volume. Rosenberg's first war poems were published in an American magazine, *Poetry* (Chicago). Some of Sassoon's poems attacking the way the war was being conducted were published in *The Cambridge Magazine*, a pacifist periodical.

✦ *Activities and discussion*

1 Sometimes the poets refer in their poems to the difficulty of writing poetry at the Front. Compare Blunden's 'Premature Rejoicing' (p. 84) with Aldington's 'Living Sepulchres' (p. 91). Can you find other poems, not necesssarily war poems, which discuss the difficulty of trying to write a poem?

143

2 Edward Thomas, in some of his earlier poems, reworked passages of his prose writing into verse. Had he lived longer, he might have done the same with material from his war diary. Read his poems carefully and decide what, for you, gives them a distinctive voice. Then aim to write a poem entitled 'No Man's Land', including some or all of the material in the following extracts from Thomas's diary of March 1917:

> Beautiful clear cloudless morning and no firing between day-break and 8. ... Linnets and chaffinches sing in waste trenched ground with trees and water tanks between us and Arras. Mag-pies over No Man's Land in pairs. The old green (grey) track crossing No Man's Land – once a country way to Arras.

> No Man's Land like Goodwood racecourse with engineers swarming over it and making a road between shell holes full of bloodstained water and beer bottles among barbed wire. Larks singing as they did when we went up in dark and were shelled. Now I hardly felt as if a shell could hurt, though several were thrown about near working parties.

What have you learned about Thomas's writing from trying to imitate it?

3 Wilfred Owen's poem 'The Sentry' (p. 42) was composed in England but was based closely on an incident which he had described in a letter written to his mother from France some months earlier.

> My own sweet Mother,
> ... I can see no excuse for deceiving you about these last 4 days.
> I have suffered seventh hell.
> I have not been at the front.
> I have been in front of it.
> I held an advanced post, that is, a 'dug-out' in the middle of 'No Man's Land'.
> We had a march of 3 miles over shelled road then nearly 3 along a flooded trench. After that we came to where the tren-

ches had been blown flat out and had to go over the top. It was of course dark, too dark, and the ground was not mud, not sloppy mud, but an octopus of sucking clay, 3, 4, and 5 feet deep, relieved only by craters full of water. Men have been known to drown in them. Many stuck in the mud & only got on by leaving their waders, equipment, and in some cases their clothes.

High explosives were dropping all round, and machine guns spluttered every few minutes. But it was so dark that even the German flares did not reveal us.

Three-quarters dead, I mean each of us 3/4 dead, we reached the dug-out, and relieved the wretches therein. I then had to go forth and and find another dug-out for a still more advanced post where I left 18 bombers. I was responsible for other posts on the left but there was a junior officer in charge.

My dug-out held 25 men tight packed. Water filled it to a depth of 1 or 2 feet, leaving say 4 feet of air.

One entrance had been blown in and blocked.

So far, the other remained.

The Germans knew we were staying there and decided we shouldn't.

Those fifty hours were the agony of my happy life.

Every ten minutes on Sunday afternoon seemed an hour. I nearly broke down and let myself drown in the water that was slowly rising over my knees.

Towards 6 o'clock, when, I suppose, you would be going to church, the shelling grew less intense and less accurate: so that I was mercifully helped to do my duty and crawl, wade, climb and flounder over No Man's Land to visit my other post. It took me half an hour to move about 150 yards.

I was chiefly annoyed by our own machine guns from behind. The seeng-seeng-seeng of the bullets reminded me of Mary's canary. On the whole I can support the canary better.

In the Platoon on my left the sentries over the dug-out were blown to nothing. One of these poor fellows was my first servant whom I rejected. If I had kept him he would have lived, for servants don't do Sentry Duty. I kept my own sentries half way down the stairs during the more terrific bombardment. In spite of this one lad was blown down and, I am afraid, blinded. This was my only casualty …

Contrast the way Owen writes this letter with the way he presents the incident in 'The Sentry'. What differences and similarities in diction and emphasis can you see? Owen was writing here for two different readers. How did this affect the way he wrote? How do you react to each piece of writing?

4 Some of the poems deliberately set out to echo ballads or the marching songs of the Great War. Read, for example, Sassoon's 'Suicide in the Trenches' (p. 60) and Blunden's 'Concert Party: Busseboom' (p. 76). Work out ways of reading these poems aloud and performing them with accompanying sound-effects, e.g. drums, trumpets, marching feet, etc. Look for other poems with strong rhythms which could be presented in this way. When you have 'performed' them, discuss how this approach helps you to enjoy or understand the poems better.

How do these poems present their subject?

✦ *Activities and discussion*

1 Never underestimate titles. They may give you valuable clues about a poem and about how you might respond to it. Compare the types of titles chosen by two or more poets: what clues do they offer? Do they help you to form an impression of how the poet thought of his poems? Edmund Blunden, for example, often used titles which were like the captions for photographs in an album. Does this mean, therefore, that readers should treat the poems as snapshots in words?

2 Several of the poems in this book present a conversation, or snatches of dialogue for more than one voice. Look, for example, at Thomas's 'As the Team's Head Brass' (p. 21), Rosenberg's 'The Dying Soldier' (p. 33), Owen's 'The Chances' (p. 42) and Aldington's 'Trench Idyll' (p. 92). Arrange for these poems to be read or acted by more than one speaker, and discuss how this way of presenting the poems helps you to understand them. Look for other poems in the book which could be performed in this way.

3 Richard Aldington was a member of the Imagist group of poets. In the preface to the anthology *Some Imagist Poets* (1915) he published the following 'Credo':
   • to use the language of common speech, but to employ always the exact word, not the nearly-exact, nor the merely decorative word;
   • to create new rhythms ... We believe that the individuality of the poet may be better expressed in free verse than in conventional forms;
   • to allow absolute freedom in the choice of subject ...
   • to present an image (hence the name 'Imagist') ... We believe that poetry should render particulars exactly and not deal in vague generalities;

- to produce poetry that is hard and clear, never blurred nor indefinite;
- finally, most of us believe that concentration is of the very essence of poetry.

Which of Aldington's own poems best reflect these Imagist principles? Choose two or three of his poems written in France and discuss whether or not these principles have made it easier for you as reader to respond to what Aldington as poet has written. Do you think there are other poems (for example by Isaac Rosenberg, or 'Ypres' by Herbert Read, p. 112) which could also be described as 'Imagist'?

4 Edmund Blunden, looking back in 1930, wrote:

> The main mystery of the Old Front Line was that it created a kind of concord between the combatants, but a discord between them and those who, not being there, kept up the war.

Which poems, not necessarily by Blunden, best illustrate this 'concord' and 'discord'?

5 In 1917, Siegfried Sassoon published the following statement:

> I am making this statement as an act of wilful defiance of military authority, because I believe that the War is being deliberately prolonged by those who have the power to end it. I am a soldier, convinced that I am acting on behalf of soldiers. I believe that this War, upon which I entered as a war of defence and liberation, has now become a war of aggression and conquest. ... I have seen and endured the sufferings of the troops, and I can no longer be a party to prolong these sufferings for ends which I believe to be evil and unjust ...

a Look again at some of Sassoon's poems in the light of this statement. How does it affect the way in which you respond to his poetry?

b As a result of making this statement, Sassoon was sent to Craiglockhart Hospital, near Edinburgh, a treatment centre for shell-shocked officers. Here he met Wilfred Owen and had a great influence on Owen's writing. He himself, however, came to feel uneasy that the only result of making his protest had been to remove him from the dangers of the Front Line. In *Sherston's Progress* (1937), Sassoon recalled how he reached the conclusion that 'going back to the War as soon as possible was my only chance of peace'. What do you think he meant by this? Do his poems help you at all to understand this paradox?

6 Some of the poems in this edition describe a complete battle or action. How different are these longer poems from those which discuss particular aspects of life in the Trenches? Look particularly at these poems:
- Isaac Rosenberg, 'Dead Man's Dump' (p. 33);
- Wilfred Owen, 'Spring Offensive' (p. 51);
- Siegfried Sassoon, 'Counter-Attack' (p. 61);
- Edmund Blunden, 'Third Ypres' (p. 80).

7 Edmund Blunden described himself at the end of *Undertones of War* as 'a harmless young shepherd in a soldier's coat'. Many of his poems, like those of Edward Thomas, show a very strong sense of the countryside. Choose two or three such poems by Blunden (and compare them with one or two by other poets) where the countryside seems as important as the war. In what sense can Blunden be described as a 'pastoral' war poet? Blunden sometimes uses traditional verse forms such as ballads. How surprising and successful do you think these verse forms are when used for war poetry?

8 For many of the poets, the mud in which they lived, fought and died became one of the most important features of their day-to-day existence; the image of a dead body lying in the mud is one of the most striking recurrent images in war

poetry. How many poems in this edition focus on the image of a dead soldier? Explore and discuss these poems to see what they have in common and how they differ from each other. Consider which of these poems you find especially memorable or effective.

✦

Who reads these poems?
How do they interpret them?

After the Great War was over, the vogue for war poetry continued for only a short period. Books such as *Counter-Attack* by Siegfried Sassoon and *Images of War* by Richard Aldington were widely read. However, for most people the most important task was to come to terms with the end of the war and the scale of the losses, both personal and national. Communities that were busy raising funds to erect war memorials did not want to be reminded of the brutal realities of the fighting in France and Belgium. It is significant that the most widely quoted poem after the war, and the one which is still quoted today at all Remembrance Day ceremonies, was 'For the Fallen' (p. 104) by Laurence Binyon, written in 1914.

A second reason why the war poets quite quickly went out of vogue was that most of them were associated with the Georgian poetry anthologies, and in the early 1920s Georgian poetry came to seem often trivial, provincial and backward-looking compared with the new, modernist writing exemplified by *The Waste Land* by T. S. Eliot. When Graves, Sassoon, Blunden and Aldington published their memoirs and novels of the First World War at the end of the 1920s, there was a renewal of interest in their poetry, but once again this was overtaken by the appearance of new writers, such as W. H. Auden who emerged in the 1930s.

When W. B. Yeats edited the *Oxford Book of Modern Verse* in 1936, he wrote in the preface, 'If war is necessary, or necessary in our time and place, it is best to forget its suffering as we do the discomfort of fever.' He refused to include any poems by Wilfred Owen in the book and effectively banished the war poets for a generation.

During the Second World War (1939–1945) the question was asked, 'Where are the war poets?', and some of the young writers caught up in the conflict very consciously looked back

to their predecessors. Keith Douglas, perhaps the most important young poet to emerge (and be killed) in the Second World
War, wrote at the end of one of his poems describing the life
of an ordinary soldier, 'Rosenberg, I only repeat what you were
saying.'

The real revival of interest in war poetry from the Great War
dates from the 1960s, when Benjamin Britten set poems by
Wilfred Owen to music in his *War Requiem* and when the
musical *Oh What a Lovely War!* used popular songs from
1914–1918 to satirise the same targets that Siegfried Sassoon
and the others had attacked fifty years earlier. Today, the place
of the war poets in the literature of the twentieth century is
being revalued by a new generation of readers, most of whom
have no direct experience of war at all, each shaping their own
responses to that remarkable range of poetry inspired by, or
created out of, the Great War. Poetry of the Great War is read
and studied in nearly all British schools; for most pupils, war
poetry is as much a part of English literature as Shakespeare.

✦ Activities and discussion

1 In 1920, the *Blue Guide to Belgium and the Western Front*
was published, and the battlefields of the Great War became
accessible to tourists and visitors. Many of these came in
search of the cemeteries where their sons, husbands or
friends had been buried; others came to explore the Trenches, ruins and other legacies of the fighting. If you were
selecting poems from the six authors in this book for visitors
to the Western Front to read, which would you choose:
   • for those who had lost family or friends during the war;
   • for those who simply wanted to explore the battlefields?

2 All six poets featured in this book were soldiers. Some of
their poems are addressed to women. Make an anthology of
these poems, and read them aloud, dramatising them where
possible.

3 In nearly every town and village in Britain there is a war memorial. Most of these were erected within three or four years of the end of the Great War. Sometimes local newspaper archives will enable you to read accounts of the dedicating of these memorials. Aim to write a short poem, in the style of either Sassoon, Blunden or Aldington, which might have been prompted by the erecting of a war memorial in their local community.

4 Choose your own favourite poem from this book, or the poem which for you best evokes the atmosphere of the Great War, and see in how many ways it can be presented. Read it aloud, if possible acting it or reading it with more than one person taking part. If it is short enough, try using it as the subject for a poster or book jacket to advertise an anthology of war poems. What sort of appropriate illustrations would help to give the poster or jacket maximum impact?

5 Siegfried Sassoon wrote about Isaac Rosenberg:

> His few but impressive 'Trench Poems' … have the controlled directness of a man finding his true voice and achieving mastery of his material; words and images obey him, instead of leading him into over-elaboration. They are all of them fine poems, but 'Break of Day in the Trenches' has for me a poignant and nostalgic quality which eliminates critical analysis. Sensuous front line existence is there, hateful and repellent, unforgettable and inescapable.

What do you think Sassoon means by a 'poignant and nostalgic quality which eliminates critical analysis'? How do his remarks affect your own response to either Rosenberg's poetry, or to the writing of other war poets?

6 Wilfred Owen drafted a preface to the book of war poems he was intending to publish:

This book is not about heroes. English poetry is not yet fit to speak of them.

Nor is it about deeds, or lands, nor anything about glory, honour, might, majesty, dominion, or power, except War.

Above all I am not concerned with Poetry.

My subject is War, and the pity of War.

The Poetry is in the pity.

Yet these elegies are to this generation in no sense consolatory. They may be to the next. All a poet can do today is warn. That is why the true Poets must be truthful.

In what ways do you find this preface useful in reading Owen's poetry? Do you think that his statements could be applied equally to each of the poets in this book?

7 In his novel *Death of a Hero* (1929), Richard Aldington wrote:

When I meet an unmaimed man of my generation, I want to shout at him: 'How did you escape? How did you dodge it? What dirty trick did you play? Why are you not dead, trickster?' It is dreadful to have outlived your life, to have shirked your fate, to have overspent your welcome … You, the war dead, I think you died in vain, I think you died for nothing, for a blast of wind, a blather, a humbug, a newspaper stunt, a politician's ramp. But at least you died … You chose the better part.

Compare this passage with some of Aldington's post-war poems, especially 'In the Palace Garden' (p. 96), 'Eumenides' (p. 97) and 'In Memory of Wilfred Owen' (p. 101). How easy do you think it would have been for readers immediately after the war to have understood Aldington's attitude? How important do you think it is for readers today to be aware of such feelings expressed by those who survived the war?

8 On the 75th anniversary of the end of the Great War, 11 November 1993, *The Times* published an editorial entitled 'History's Trenches'. It contained this argument:

This week, millions of Britons will wear a poppy with pride. Yet many – perhaps most – will do so quite convinced that the Great War was a futile waste of life in which lions were led to the slaughter by donkeys. Few historical orthodoxies have proved so resilient or been so well popularised ... Literature has played a central role in the perpetuation of this orthodoxy. Few educated people in this country cannot quote a few lines from Wilfred Owen's anti-war poems. Few books set in battle have been so popular as Siegfried Sassoon's *Memoirs of an Infantry Officer*, Robert Graves's *Goodbye to All That* or Erich Maria Remarque's *All Quiet on the Western Front*. Unlike the Second World War, the First produced a distinct literary aesthetic, rooted in a sense of futility and betrayal. Because this orthodoxy is so settled, it should be questioned all the more vigorously.

How does this argument affect or challenge the way you respond to the war poems in this book?

✦

FURTHER READING

The list of books that follows will give you some idea of where to look first if you want to find out more about each of the six poets in this book, or about the way writers and others have shaped our ideas about the Great War.

Edward Thomas

G. Thomas (ed.), *The Collected Poems of Edward Thomas* (Oxford University Press, 1981)

This edition contains an introduction and a chronology of Edward Thomas's life, together with notes on the poems and his diary entries in the weeks leading up to his death.

Jan Marsh, *Edward Thomas: a Poet for his Country* (Paul Elek, 1978)

There have been several biographies of Edward Thomas, and this is an indication of his growing importance as a figure in twentieth-century literature. Jan Marsh's book is particularly good at describing Thomas's growth as a poet, and his friendship with other poets before and during the Great War.

Isaac Rosenberg

Gordon Bottomley & Denys Harding (eds), *The Collected Poems of Isaac Rosenberg* (Chatto & Windus, 1949)

This edition contains all of Rosenberg's poems and verse plays. It has a preface by Siegfried Sassoon.

Joseph Cohen, *Journey to the Trenches: the Life of Isaac Rosenberg 1890–1918* (Robson, 1975)

Rosenberg's struggle against poverty and his determination to succeed both as a poet and as an artist are well described in this book, which also has an interesting final chapter on the way his reputation has taken so long to become established.

Wilfred Owen

Jon Stallworthy (ed.), *The Poems of Wilfred Owen* (Chatto & Windus, 1990)

This is the standard edition of Owen's poetry, and is particularly useful for the way it explains how nearly every poem was drafted, revised and made ready for the book of war poems which Owen never lived to see published. The introduction and notes are very thorough.

Jon Stallworthy, *Wilfred Owen* (Oxford University Press, 1974)

Dominic Hibberd, *Wilfred Owen: the Last Year* (Constable, 1992)

Jon Stallworthy's biography of Owen presents a very detailed and sympathetic picture of the poet's life. Dominic Hibberd's later book gives an almost day-by-day account of Owen's last year – the year which saw him find his full voice as a poet.

Siegfried Sassoon

Siegfried Sassoon, *Collected Poems 1908–1956* (Faber, 1984)

Siegfried Sassoon, *Complete Memoirs of George Sherston* (Faber, 1937)

It is curious that not more has been written about Sassoon. His *Complete Memoirs*, which includes *Memoirs of a Foxhunting Man* and *Memoirs of an Infantry Officer*, gives a detailed picture of his life before and during the war, but it is a mistake to assume that it is straightforward autobiography: George Sherston is not identical to Siegfried Sassoon in every respect, not least because the books never suggest that Sherston is a poet as well as a soldier. A recent novel about Sassoon (Pat Barker, *Regeneration*, Penguin, 1993) gives a remarkable insight into his experiences at Craiglockhart during the war.

Edmund Blunden

Edmund Blunden: Poems of Many Years (Collins, 1957)

This selection was edited by Rupert Hart-Davis. A more recent edition, *Edmund Blunden: Selected Poems* (ed. Robyn Marsack, Carcanet, 1982) contains an excellent introduction, a chronology and notes.

Edmund Blunden, *Undertones of War* (Penguin, 1982)

This book, first published in 1928, contains both Blunden's memoir of the war, based on the diaries that he kept, and a number of war poems written after 1918.

Barry Webb, *Edmund Blunden, a Biography* (Yale, 1990)

The chapters in this biography dealing with Blunden's career during the Great War fill in many of the gaps left in *Undertones of War*, gaps caused by Blunden's own reticence.

Richard Aldington

Richard Aldington, *Complete Poems* (Alan Wingate, 1948)

There is no recent edition of Aldington's poetry, although there has been a marked revival of interest in his work during the past ten years. Some of his war poems can be found in anthologies, including *Lads: Love Poetry of the Trenches* (ed. Martin Taylor, Constable, 1989). His novel *Death of a Hero* has been recently re-issued, and Charles Doyle's biography is important in placing Aldington as a major figure in the literary life of the century.

Richard Aldington, *Death of a Hero* (Chatto & Windus, 1929)

Richard Aldington, *At All Costs* (Imperial War Museum, 1992)

Charles Doyle, *Richard Aldington* (Macmillan, 1989)

Further Poems

The following anthologies will be helpful in broadening your experience of the poetry of the Great War:

Dominic Hibberd & John Onions (eds), *Poetry of the Great War* (Macmillan, 1986)

Tim Cross, *The Lost Voices of World War I* (Bloomsbury, 1988)

Tim Cross's valuable book contains brief biographies and critical introductions to writers from all sides who were killed in the Great War.

Catherine Reilly (ed.), *Scars Upon My Heart* (Virago, 1981)

Nora Jones & Liz Ward (eds), *The Forgotten Army* (Highgate Publications, 1991)

Both these books set out to demonstrate the range of poetry written by women during the Great War. *The Forgotten Army* contains excellent contemporary photographs to accompany the poems.

Jon Silkin, *Out of Battle* (Ark, 1987)

Elizabeth A. Marsland, *The Nation's Cause: English, French and German Poetry of the First World War* (Routledge, 1991)

Two important critical guides to the poetry of the Great War.

Paul Fussell, *The Great War and Modern Memory* (Oxford University Press, 1975)

Samuel Hynes, *A War Imagined: the First World War and English Culture* (Pimlico, 1992)

Both these books provide exciting and thought-provoking discussions of the way the Great War has acquired almost mythical significance in the twentieth century. Each book contains extended discussions of the poetry of Siegfried Sassoon, and Paul Fussell also writes at length about Edmund Blunden. Samuel Hynes explores the way in which a writer such as Richard Aldington is able to look ahead, even during the heat of battle, to a time in which the war will have become only a memory. Both books are essential reading for anyone who wants to explore the poetry of the Great War in a wider cultural context.

✦

Acknowledgements

The editor is grateful to Mrs Claire Blunden for her guidance on the dating of poems by Edmund Blunden, and to David Wilkinson for biographical and bibliographical information about the poems of Richard Aldington.

The author and publishers would like to thank the following for permission to reproduce copyright material:

p. 38 '1914' and 'Nocturne', p. 39 'Anthem for Doomed Youth', p. 40 'Dulce et Decorum Est', p. 41 'The Next War', p. 42 'The Chances' and 'The Sentry', p. 44 'Exposure', p. 48 'Strange Meeting', p. 51 'Spring Offensive' from *The Poems of Wilfred Owen* (Chatto and Windus, 1990), edited by Jon Stallworthy, courtesy of The Hogarth Press and the Estate of Wilfred Owen; p. 54 'A Letter Home', p. 56 'The Hero', p. 57 'A Working Party', p. 58 'The General' and 'Base Details', p. 59 'Song-Books of the War', p. 60 'Suicide in the Trenches' and 'The Dug-Out', p. 62 'Glory of Women', p. 63 'Sick Leave', p. 65 'Everyone Sang' and 'To One Who Was With Me in the War', p. 67 'On Passing the New Menin Gate' by Siegfried Sassoon, by permission of George Sassoon; p. 70 'Festubert: the Old German Line' and 'The Unchangeable', p. 71 'Les Halles d'Ypres' and 'Reunion in War', p. 74 'The Sentry's Mistake', p. 75 'The Zonnebeke Road', p. 76 'Concert Party: Busseboom', p. 77 'Vlamertinghe: Passing the Château, July 1917', p. 78 'Report on Experience' and 'Illusions', p. 79 'The Ancre at Hamel: Afterwards', p. 80 'Third Ypres', p. 84 'Premature Rejoicing', p. 85 'Can You Remember?', p. 86 'To W.O. and his Kind' by Edmund Blunden, reprinted by permission of the Peters, Fraser and Dunlop Group Ltd; p. 88 'Sunsets' and 'Field Manoeuvres', p. 89 'Soliloquy', p. 90 'Picket', p. 91 'Bombardment' and 'Living Sepulchres', p. 92 'Reserve' and 'Trench Idyll', p. 93 'In the Trenches', p. 94 'Meditation', p. 96 'In the Palace Garden', p. 97 'Eumenides', p. 99 'Epilogue to Death of a Hero', p. 101 'In Memory of Wilfred Owen' by Richard Aldington © The Estate of Richard Aldington; p. 107 'Easter Monday' by Eleanor Farjeon from *First and Second Love* published by Oxford University Press, reprinted by permission of David Higham Associates; p. 108 'Picnic' by Rose Macaulay, reprinted by permission of the Peters, Fraser and Dunlop Group Ltd; p. 111 'A Dead Boche' by Robert Graves from *Poems about War*, reprinted by permission of A. P. Watt Ltd on behalf of the Trustees of the Robert Graves Copyright Trust; p. 113 'Lament' by W. W. Gibson, by permission of Macmillan London Ltd; p. 114 from 'Hugh Selwyn Mauberley' by Ezra Pound (PERSONAE). Copyright © 1926 by Ezra Pound. Reprinted by permission of Faber and Faber Ltd and New Directions Publishing Corp.

Every effort has been made to reach copyright holders; the publishers would like to hear from anyone whose rights they have unknowingly infringed.